EDITH ~ EDDIE

The Good, Bad, and Ugly Truth
The Story of An Oscar-Nominated Documentary

Patricia Barber
Edith H Initiative LLC

Copyright © 2025 Patricia Barber

All rights reserved

No part of this book may be reproduced, distributed, or transmitted in any form or by any means, including photocopying, recording, or other electronic or mechanical methods, without the prior written permission of the publisher, except in the case of quotations used in reviews or critical articles.

This is a work of nonfiction based on actual events and real individuals. The events described reflect the author's personal experiences, recollections, and interpretations; while every effort has been made to ensure accuracy, certain details may be reconstructed from memory.

For permissions, contact:
Patricia Barber

ISBN: 979-8-9932978-0-4

Cover design owned by: Keith Cullings Jr.

Independently published

Printed in the United States of America

Dedication

This book is dedicated to our many seniors across the nation who, through no fault of their own, fall victim to abuse of various kinds (physical, emotional, financial, etc.) Statistics show an ongoing need to protect our seniors thru nationwide agencies, including our justice department, senior advocates, protective services agencies, media coverage, exposure, and most importantly our family members. It is especially important to recognize all aspects of our senior's vulnerabilities. Aging is a continuous process that requires ongoing attention, care, and adaptation to the body's shifting needs. Often our seniors are viewed through a blind eye lens and their needs overlooked and cast aside. The documentary entitled Edith + Eddie is an example of how a film can promote a misconstrued narrative. If you have already seen the film, you may believe it is, above all, a tale of love. However, beneath the thin romantic surface lies a much more complex story. It fails to delve into the deeper reality of one person's struggle with dementia and the other's vulnerability amid the challenges of aging. A few family members, strangers, and even a celebrity were instrumental in moving this story to monumental heights. But the truth of the matter is a story I am compelled to tell. Films can capture emotion, but they rarely capture everything. What began as a search for understanding became a pursuit of truth. The unspoken moments often tell the truest version of events. In this book, that is what I have done. These chapters will explore the events leading up to Edith and Eddie's meeting, the period during which the documentary was filmed, and the aftermath following its release and subsequent award nominations. This book presents the facts surrounding the circumstances of Edith and Eddie. Supporting documents have been included to confirm the events, legal judgments, and corresponding dates. My goal is for you to be able to see through the carefully crafted fairytale that Edith + Eddie, the documentary, presented to the public.

Contents

01	Blindfolded	1
02	Heart Strings	5
03	My Valve to You	7
04	Scar Tissue	9
05	Family Heartbreak	23
06	Hearts Are Red	31
07	Blood Is Blue	44
08	Circulation	50
09	Breathe Without Air	54
10	Edith + Eddie	60
11	The Circulatory System	76
12	Family Anatomy	80
13	Heart of War	83
	Sources	86
	Appendix	87

01

Blindfolded

Adults over the age of 80 years old are most likely to suffer from elder abuse. According to the National Council on Aging (NCOA), nearly 50% of people with dementia suffer from elder abuse and neglect. There are many signs of elder abuse: physical, emotional, sexual, financial, abandonment, and neglect. Each carry a different set of warning signs, along with over lapping signs from one to the others. Some warning signs can be difficult to spot, while others are more obvious. Nonetheless, overlooking them can prove to be a mistake. It is on record that multibillions are lost in the United States each year at the hands of elder financial abusers.

According to the Department of Justice:

Civil Financial Exploitation 10 G.C.A. 21002

Financial or Property Exploitation – means illegal or improper use of an elderly or adult with a disability's money, property, or other resources for monetary or personal benefit, profit or gain. This includes, but is not limited to, theft, misappropriation, concealment, misuse or fraudulent deprivation of money or property belonging to the elderly or adult with a disability. Adult with a Disability – is any person eighteen (18) years or older who: 1. Has a physical or mental impairment which substantially limits one or more major life activities; or has a history of, or has been classified as having, an impairment which substantially limits one or more major life activities.

Elderly – refers to a person aged sixty (60) years or older.

Civil Financial Exploitation 22 M.R.S 3472

Exploitation – means the illegal or improper use of an incapacitated or dependent adult or that adult's resources for another's profit or advantage. Incapacitated adult – means an adult who is unable to receive and evaluate information or make or communicate informed decisions to such an extent that the adult lacks the ability to meet essential requirements for physical health, safety or self-care, even with reasonably available appropriate technological assistance.

Warning Signs of Physical Abuse:

- Bruises, black eyes, welts, lacerations, or rope marks
- Bone fractures, broken bones, or skull fractures
- Open wounds, cuts, punctures, untreated injuries in various stages of healing
- Sprains, dislocations, or internal injuries/bleeding
- Broken eyeglasses/frames, physical signs of being subjected to punishment, or signs of being restrained.
- Laboratory findings of medication overdose **or under-utilization of prescribed drugs**
- An older adult's sudden change in behavior
- The caregiver's **refusal to allow visitors to see an older adult alone**
- An older adult's report of being hit, slapped, kicked, or mistreated

Warning Signs of Financial Exploitation:

- Sudden changes in bank accounts or banking practices, including an **unexplained withdrawal of large sums of money** by a person accompanying the older adult
- The **inclusion of additional names** on an older adult's bank signature card

- Unauthorized withdrawal of the older adult's funds using their ATM card
- Abrupt **changes in a will** or other financial documents
- Unexplained **disappearance of funds or valuable possessions**
- Provision of substandard care or bills left unpaid despite the availability of adequate financial resources
- Discovery of a forged signature for financial transactions or for the titles of the older adult's possessions
- Sudden appearance of previously uninvolved relatives **claiming their rights to an older adult's property or possessions**
- Unexplained sudden transfer of assets to a family member or someone outside the family
- The provision of services that are not necessary
- An older adult's report of financial exploitation

Warning Signs of Neglect and Abandonment:
- **Dehydration, malnutrition**, untreated bed sores, and poor personal hygiene
- Unattended or **untreated health problems**
- **Hazardous or unsafe living conditions/** arrangements (e.g., improper wiring, no heat, or no running water)
- Unsanitary and unclean living condition (e.g., dirt, fleas, lice on person, soiled bedding, fecal/urine smell, inadequate clothing)
- The **desertion of an older adult at a hospital**, a nursing facility, or other similar institution, or a shopping center or other public location
- An older adult's report of being neglected or abandoned.

The warning signs shown in bold mirror the very behaviors I witnessed in my sister's actions. According to other sources, transferring power of attorney or changing a will when an adult is no longer capable of deciding for themselves can likewise be indicators of exploitation. There is also sudden weight loss, which can stem from a variety of reasons but should never be overlooked. Be aware of all the signs, there are many more online.

Elderly people who fall victim to financial exploitation and abuse pay a price that goes well beyond money. As you see, the added emotional despair they also endure as a result of these actions can levy heavy consequences for them. A group of trusted family members should keep a close watch on those providing care to their elderly relatives. Detailed records of everything should be kept with backup copies stored within the trusted group. I never recommend relying on one person to do the heavy lifting. It takes a village. Reach out to one of the many government agencies if you suspect an elder family member of being abused.

02
Heart Strings

I am Patricia Barber, the youngest daughter of Edith Hill. Let me begin by saying may Mom & Eddie rest in eternal peace. The real story is compelling enough to be a Hollywood movie. My sister Rebecca has put me in a difficult position: I must reveal what truly happened while also showing compassion for Eddie, who was taken advantage of and, unfortunately, I could not save.

They say the camera never lies, yet the story of my mother and Eddie was only partially revealed. They were taken advantage of quietly while the world watched. This book is my attempt to shine light on the part of the story left in the shadows and to honor the lasting legacy of my mother.

I sincerely hope others will benefit from exposing the verifiable truth surrounding the elders and prevent further injustices to other seniors. "Edith + Eddie" tells the story of two people who supposedly found love late in life. A real tearjerker as viewed and described by many.

Sadly, the story as viewed contained much misleading information. In actuality, the legalities of the marriage were unclear due to mysterious circumstances. The real story involves power, unprecedented privilege, and elder exploitation. This award-winning documentary is deceptive with its contents. The Director chose not to exercise her right to obtain the complete story in the development of the documentary. The results produced a one-sided story. Many film festivals declared the story a winner of over 30 awards.

Professionals from various backgrounds viewed, critiqued, and voted adding to the elevation and promotion of the documentary. This ultimately led to the production receiving **Oscar** and **Emmy** nominations.

03
My Valve to You

(My Vow to You)

Edith Hill

Edith, whose family name is Hubbard, was the mother of four children; Lewis, Ernestine (Tina), Rebecca, and Patricia all fathered by Lewis McDaniel. Edith married at an early age to Mr. McDaniel which ended in divorce. She was often described as a sweet, kind, caring, giving, and loving person who lived a very private life and conquered many challenges through her strong faith and religious beliefs. Her second marriage to Mr. Hill facilitated the relocation of her family from Christiansburg, Virginia to Alexandria, Virginia where together they purchased the home which is featured in the documentary. Edith practiced her religious beliefs daily and always focused on Church and family. Mr. Hill passed in the early 1960's leaving Ms. Hill a widow. Ms. Hill continued to live in her home in Alexandria, Virginia.

Edith spent over the next forty years as a widow. In her early seventies Edith welcomed her long-time male companion, Henry, for the next 18 years. Her long-term live-in relationship with Henry ended when he faced health issues, and she could no longer provide him with suitable care. As Edith continued to age it became clear that her children would need to intervene and provide suitable care as required. Edith's son, Lewis, moved in with her in mid-2000.

Eddie Harrison

Around 2007, Eddie met Edith along with my brother Lewis at a 7 Eleven. They engaged in conversation and became friends. According to my brother, their first conversation mainly involved Eddie detailing how he lost his wife. As the weeks passed, Edith offered him a number to play. He did so and eventually won. That is when he gave $250 to Edith and $250 to Lewis. Because of this friendship, that is ultimately how Eddie met Rebecca.

After the recent loss of his previous wife to dementia, Eddie vowed to never marry again as he said it would ruin his retirement. At 92-years-old in 2011, he struggled with numerous health issues including a significant loss of hearing. Eddie's known relatives were a niece and nephew of distant kinship, both in their eighties; he had no children of his own. Eddie lived alone and rented from his nephew. Due to Eddie's physical needs and his lack of transportation it became difficult for him to maneuver.

Eddie's need for around-the-clock care quickly approached as he continued to age. Eddie fell ill to a sickness causing him to land in a nursing home for quite some time. Without any real support system, his ageing nephew and niece encouraged him to stay in the nursing home long term. That was not Eddie's desire, so he left. He became a perfect target for deceitful scams, including exploitation. Eddie's vulnerability unfortunately came to fruition.

04

Scar Tissue

Rebecca, the third child of four, was always a rebel. Prankster, a good way to describe her childhood. There is a three-year difference between us. When she was graduating high school, I was just beginning. She was an employee in the Fairfax County school system. She married an attorney who graduated from Harvard law school. With that relationship, she learned how to maneuver through situations where others may have needed legal representation. She was privy to the ins and outs of the court system. Over a few decades she began acquiring assets, I believed like anyone else would about a sibling, that my sister was advancing in the world. There was no proof of wrongdoing, so I did not consider looking into any of her actions. On top of that, we lived in different states.

I took time to reflect, look over all her actions, interviewed family members, and realized that she had been manipulating people for a long time. Her strange actions repeated over and over, she has a way with words, and always seemed to position herself around elders in need. Over a decade ago my brother Lewis cautioned me of the potential challenges I would face with Rebecca. Let's walk back in time...

A Brother's Warning

My brother Lewis was the oldest of the bunch. Our relationship wasn't the strongest. There were no problems, just the age difference of 8 years made our communication distant. He was grown and trying to live out his life. I was a kid still going through the motions. Lewis was the first to begin taking care of Mom. He assumed the responsibilities to ensure her wellbeing.

My phone rang back-to-back, I received calls from both Lewis and Rebecca. Both wanted to share their concerns relating to Mom's specific needs and care. Lewis was overly concerned that Mom's Will had been changed by Rebecca. We set up a meeting at Mom's address. All four siblings were in attendance. We were unable to locate the original Will, leaving the matter unresolved.

Rebecca contacted Adult Protective Services accusing Lewis of physically abusing Mom. Similar malicious accusations were made against my husband in the documentary. Rebecca continued to take control of Mom and her assets. Unfortunately, Mom would sign any paperwork given to her. The papers were drawn up by Rebecca's lawyer connections. Power of attorney, bank accounts, retirement beneficiaries, and insurance beneficiaries were all a part of the paperwork drafted. In an attempt to take control, Rebecca managed to take Mom to the bank and withdraw money from one of her accounts. That specific account Mom shared with my brother Lewis. Rebecca then opened a new checking account jointly in her name and Mom's.

One day Lewis took Mom to the bank to make a withdrawal to pay for her medicine, they both were unaware of the changes made by Rebecca. Mom was told by the teller at the bank that she did not have any money, "Your daughter took your money." Mom was totally devastated and repeatedly stated that she could not believe one of her children would do such a thing. Mom's savings account was also altered, with Rebecca added as a joint account holder. Lewis continued to live with Mom and resist the pressure and interference from Rebecca. All pleas and attempts to persuade Rebecca to return Mom's money were met with refusal. Rebecca did not speak to Mom for at least a year, leaving Lewis to hold her together throughout that entire time.

Meanwhile, Lewis and I continued to comfort Mom and reassure her that Protective Services was involved and she would soon have her money returned. Lewis worked closely with Protective Services assuring that all Power of Attorney's were revoked, and he was designated as Mom's Representative Payee. Lewis became ill which caused another round of concerns for Mom. It became clear that both Lewis and Mom would need additional assistance as they aged.

Lewis had a close friend, John, who helped with upkeep and maintenance around the house who also proved to be very attentive to Mom. John called Mom "Mama." Lewis's separated wife was hired by my sister Tina for light meals and hygiene purposes. We all chipped in to keep Mom comfortable. I purchased a replacement kitchen stove and arranged for "meals on wheels" to be delivered.

Meanwhile, Rebecca continued to file complaints with Protective Services. A clerk said there were over 20 claims against Lewis and his family. In an effort to get away, Lewis made the trip from Northern Virginia to my Baltimore home, accompanied by Mom and her "friend," Eddie. The trip served multiple purposes: Lewis wanted to introduce me to Eddie, spend time with me, and escape the mounting stress. Eddie appeared to be a thoughtful person, bringing a gift for my young grandson. I was not surprised at their friendship; Mom was a very friendly kind of person also.

My long-awaited move to Florida was completed in June 2009. Again, believing all is well with Mom proved to be the beginning of many unexpected challenges.

Once more, I began to receive phone calls from both Lewis and Rebecca. Mom is now ninety-one years old exhibiting many symptoms relating to dementia. The time the seniors spent together was extremely limited and dependent on Lewis for transportation.

Ongoing discontent continued over the next years, especially when Lewis's daughter Lois and her family needed a place to stay. Without hesitation, Mom welcomed her granddaughter Lois and her family, consisting of her husband, and stepdaughter who also had a daughter. Rebecca once more filed reports to APS.

Back in 2004, Rebecca also objected to a young male cousin moving in the home. Mitchel lived in the basement for a while and proved to be helpful. This was someone to be in the house with Mom at night.

Rebecca made vicious attempts to remove Lois, her niece, from Mom's home. Rebecca would call me daily with a variety of complaints referencing Lois living in the house. Insisting that Mom was being used, taken advantage of monetarily, and including physical strain. At this point I did not know which sibling to believe. Since reports had been filed against Lewis, and now his daughter, I was being led to believe that Rebecca was looking out for Mom's best interest. I could not confirm anything through phone conversations with Mom due to her dementia progression. Lewis adamantly denied information passed along to me from Rebecca.

This new round of complaints against Lewis's daughter Lois opened new probes into the situation. APS would complete two investigations, one for Lewis and one for Lois and her family. Each day Rebecca would report to me incidents that were happening at the house one after another.

Rebecca claimed Mom was robbed. She stated that her social security card, driver's license, and a few gold coins were all missing. Rebecca went as far as to say gasoline was being siphoned from Mom's vehicle. She mentioned Mom's sleep was being disturbed by late in/out family activities, while also leaving their two-year-old grandbaby for Mom to watch. It gets ugly when she makes the claim that she found a crack pipe in the basement, and reported that the outside shed was full of stolen goods.

Rebecca confronted Lois demanding she and her family to "get out!" Having concern for Mom's wellbeing, I made a trip to Virginia to visit the home hoping to unravel some of the "he said, she said." While visiting, I found a bag of women's blouses and sweaters. As I examined them, I also found a mini waist band pocketbook. I continued to unzip the zippers, and voila, I found Mom's driver's license. I asked Rebecca where the bag of clothes came from, she said that she had given them to Mom previously. My suspicions were elevated. Rebecca also planned to have a lease drawn and have Mom sign it to force Lois and her family out of the home.

On a trip to the bank with Mom, Lewis inquired about a lockbox that had been opened with Mom's name on it. He asked if Mom could look at the contents. Mom walked out with her supposedly stolen social security card and other papers. The lockbox had been provided by the bank when Mom's accounts were being changed. And who was involved with that?! Rebecca.

A Mother's Wishes

After receiving numerous complaints from Rebecca and multiple investigations concerning the wellbeing of Mom, Adult Protective Services turned the case over to the court system. They would run multiple investigations responding to these complaints, but nothing of significance was found. The turmoil and "sibling" rivalry had become a nuisance for the case workers. While Rebecca was filing these complaints against Lewis, she simultaneously took Mom to the doctors. Her goal in doing so was to petition the Court to become Mom's guardian but Rebecca needed proof validating Mom's condition.

In January 2011, the neurologist revealed Mom had significant loss of function in multiple domains of cognition. Her mental examination score was 12/30 which is consistent with a moderate degree of dementia.[1] In addition, her MRI revealed moderate cortical atrophy and small vessel disease consistent with Alzheimer's disease or arteriosclerotic dementia.

An Ad-litem was instructed to go out to evaluate Mom before her Court date. It was in that report that Mom told the Ad-litem that she did not want Rebecca to control any of her assets. She went as far to say, "please don't let me go with Rebecca." After changing her Will, emptying her bank account of $11,000 and refusing to return the funds, Mom objected to Rebecca becoming her guardian.

With these new revelations, Rebecca did not show up to the hearing. Before she was susceptible to manipulation and long before any documentary, Mom was privy to the things Rebecca was capable of doing. Mom literally shed tears for an entire year over the things Rebecca had done.[2] At the time it was hard for me to pinpoint the source of the issues between Rebecca, Lewis, and Mom. But with a little dementia and a little charm, Rebecca was able to maneuver back into Mom's good graces years later.

Tina's Troubles

Due to Rebecca's actions, the court sent out two different ad-litem to interview Lewis and Mom. The ad-litem generated through APS interviewed Lewis and did not recommend him to the courts.[3] The ad-litem sent out through Rebecca's attorney reported Mom's request of not wanting to be with Rebecca, to the court.[5] Although Lewis was not recommended, he still hired an attorney for the court hearing. Following the court decision to declare Mom incompetent, Lewis, Tina, and I proceeded to that attorney's office to finalize paperwork. Because Rebecca was a no show for Mom's court hearing, she was not a part of any conversations pertaining to guardianship therefore eliminating her from this process. Tina volunteered, applied, and was awarded guardianship. She qualified being the oldest daughter, lived alone, close in proximity, and had good credit worthiness.[6]

In August of 2011, the court of Alexandria Virginia officially declared mom an incapacitated adult unable to handle her business affairs. This marks the beginning of Mom's life changing dramatically. She was confused about the whole situation. I previously had a one-on-one talk with her trying to explain what was going on. Everything was a whirlwind. After the court awarded guardianship to Tina, Mom and Lewis continued to live in her primary residence for a couple months.

Eventually, with the court's intervention, Mom's money and accounts were transferred over to Tina from Rebecca. The spotlight and focus then shifted to Tina, which highlighted many new negative accusations. Tina's troubles with Rebecca stem from the perceived mishandling of Mom's money and medicals.

When mom physically moved to Maryland to live with Tina in late 2011, Rebecca's complaints escalated. Those targeted criticisms began immediately within the first 6 months of Tina's guardian responsibilities. For the second time I found myself in the same position of not truly knowing which sibling was telling the truth. Rebecca also believed that Tina did not do enough to keep up with Mom's hygiene and social wellbeing. Nor did she believe Tina kept up with Mom's property.

Lewis Sent to A Nursing Home

The year 2012 proved to be even more devasting with many unpredictable changes and challenges for our family. Lewis was diagnosed with a severe illness. As Lewis's need for daily care increased (difficulty walking, diet, etc.), and with doctors' recommendations, Lewis was admitted to a nursing home for the care he needed. It became increasingly clear that time would be a factor in his recovery and release. Rebecca immediately presented herself to the staff as an overly concerned sister. Lewis was always happy to have a visitor but remained suspect of Rebecca's true motives.

Tina hesitated at a request from Lewis to bring Mom from Baltimore to Virginia for a visit in the nursing home. This was very upsetting and worrisome for him. Even though I was able to visit him twice, in early January 2012, I let him know that Rebecca could get to him quicker if he had an emergency because she was close in proximity. Meanwhile, Rebecca promised and planned a birthday party with the staff of the nursing home for Lewis. This was to be the last week of January of 2012.

But in true form, Rebecca was a no show with her party plans, baffling the staff and others. She had stopped coming around leading all the way up to the party. As Lewis got more ill, Rebecca came back around to visit, but Lewis became even more suspicious. He asked me to call him every night around 10pm for conversation. He told me whenever he left for therapy, he noticed that his personal belongings had been tampered with. He suspected Rebecca was snooping around and asked me to have my husband stop by the nursing home. Like something out of a movie, my husband was tasked with retrieving Lewis's and Mom's papers and delivering them to me in Florida. My husband often traveled to Virginia to visit his own family.

We continued to talk every night when he told me that Rebecca had presented him with a Power of Attorney form completed and ready for his signature. Under pressure from the facility to switch to Medicaid, which would take over his assets to pay for his care, he asked me to check the ins and outs of the program. Under the guise of trying to protect Lewis's assets from Medicaid, Rebecca showed immaculate timing in offering to take over. But clearly, he had quite a bit of mistrust in Rebecca and did not want her to become his POA.

Before entering the Medicaid program, we discussed an insurance policy in which he would not be able to pay the premium. I offered to pay his monthly premium with the stipulation that "when you getti-up out of here, you'll have to pay me back." We laughed. His daughter Lois was the primary beneficiary with Mom as the second beneficiary. No strings attached. His daughter eventually received the benefits. As time went on Lewis continued to weaken. My husband and I visited Lewis in the next month and took him out of the nursing home to a shopping center for an outing. After that, when I returned home in Florida, I received a call from the nursing home informing me that Lewis had gone to the Administrative Office to make me his POA. Our calls continued every night at 10pm.

In April of 2012, tragedy struck as Lewis has passed. In the hospital at our brother's death bed, Rebecca had one last thing to say to Lewis's daughter Lois. "Your mother is gone, your daddy is gone, you are on your own now." An insensitive statement to make to our niece.

Eddie, Tina (Sister), Brianna (My Grandniece), Edith (Mom), Lewis (Brother)

I took a flight to Northern Virginia and met Lois at the funeral home. We made our way to the nursing home to collect his belongings, only to be stunned to find that someone had already taken his personal possessions. We called the police to make a report. Baffled by the situation, we discover that Rebecca was the culprit. We were informed that without proof she could say he gave his belongings to her.

Included in the papers that Lewis sent to me, was the title to a vehicle co-owned by Mom and Lewis. The title had terms of "survivorship" which means that Mom owned the car at his passing. Lewis had previously loaned the car to his daughter and her husband because he could no longer drive. I made sure to give the registration and title to Lois to place it in the glove compartment.

We drove to the funeral home the next day to view his body before cremation. Rebecca had called into the funeral home to get a heads up to when we would be there. She camped out at the top of a hill and stalked us upon our arrival. We were confronted by Rebecca alleging she owned the car, and we better not move it. She bent over with a screw driver to remove the tags saying that she had paid Tina for the car, and it was hers. Since Tina was the Guardian/Conservator of Mom at this moment, and Mom technically owned the car, we had no idea any business dealings were made. Rebecca dared Lois and her family to get in the vehicle.

I asked her to show me the paperwork with tags to replace the ones on the car. When she failed to show me any valid paperwork or tags to properly move the car from the funeral home, I told Lois and her husband to leave with the car. All this commotion over a car was going on as our brother was laid out behind a curtain. I had to remind Rebecca where she was and that I would call the police.

The Funeral Director asked that I not call the authorities to his establishment. Because Lois was my ride to the Airport, he offered to drive me there. Like a scene out of a fatal attraction movie, my sister Rebecca started to follow us. The Funeral Director looked at me and said, "She ain't going to trail us." So mid-way there we pull into an alley of a Fish Market to hide until she passed by. The stench of fish in the air added to the drama of it all. It felt like we were there for hours, it was only a few minutes. The only thing missing was dramatic music. After the adrenaline rush, we proceeded to Dulles where I made my way back to Florida.

Now back in Florida, about two weeks later, I received a call from the Police informing me of an incident. They let me know that the car had been impounded. Rebecca had reported the car stolen. Lewis's daughter Lois and her husband were pulled over at gunpoint with their two-year old granddaughter in the car. The car now impounded, left Lewis's daughter and her granddaughter standing on the street and her husband in jail. Luckily, my husband was in the area at his niece's wedding and drove over to pick them up. Rebecca had the audacity to believe she owned the car because she wrote Tina a check for the purchase of the car. But when Tina turned the check over to her lawyer who was assisting with Mom's finances, the transaction was incomplete due to the check being incorrectly dated. Rebecca claimed she was testing Tina's intelligence, admitting the check was dated a year earlier. Just another prank under the belt of Rebecca to add to the nuisance she was becoming. Not to mention the chaotic scene she caused at the funeral home when she never even paid for the vehicle.

Fast forward a week, Tina sent Mom to Lewis's funeral with a caregiver, and Rebecca did not attend. The timing is ambiguous, but at some point Rebecca managed in a short period of visitation with Mom, to retrieve the car from the impound lot. It was in those small windows of opportunity that Rebecca took advantage of Tina's kindness. Rebecca needed Mom's signature in order to gain possession of the car. To this day, I do not know if Rebecca ever officially paid for the car. The signs were always there. You cannot ignore people's actions even if they are family. Those actions will become increasingly worse.

Unfortunate Circumstances

Taking care of Mom proved to be overwhelming for Tina. The emotional strain Rebecca was causing in combination with round-the-clock care was exhausting. In the midst of this, some relatives were wondering what I was doing, not knowing how involved I had been from afar. So I offered my support to my sister to have our mother visit Florida.

Around May of 2012, Mom takes a vacation. She would stay in Florida for the next 8 months. We would go to visit local churches and beaches in the area. This set the foundation of some familiarity for her. Mom was able to reunite with some of her grandsons and great grandsons. We all spent time reminiscing of the memories we had. She could recall some memories, while others she struggled with. Nonetheless, it was still a good experience for her and family. When relatives would call, they asked Mom "how are you doing?" her reply would be "I'm living the life of Riley."

While Mom was having fun and enjoying the sun, Rebecca was continuing her rampage of complaints against Tina. The concerns over Mom's money were non-stop. Through a source unknown, Rebecca was able to generate a report of how Tina spent our mother's funds. This report landed in my hands where I was able to review the accounting for myself. I will admit seeing the report with my own two eyes was a little alarming. For the first time I could see Rebecca had a legitimate concern.

In this window of time (May 2012 – December 2012), Mom began a routine of medical evaluations with doctors in Florida. I wanted to make sure she was evaluated properly and in good condition, as some days she would appear faint. At that particular time I attributed it to old age and being drained by the changes taking place in her life. Once the doctors started performing examinations, I inquired about a lump I noticed on her breast. Mom was officially diagnosed with breast cancer. Another enormous blow to the health of our mother as we already knew the other aliments she was experiencing. I questioned Tina and Rebecca about whether they knew a lump was there, both said they did, both expressed a nonchalant concern.

Upon these new revelations, Tina's lawyer stated that Mom must return to Maryland immediately. Although I was comfortable caring for her, the lawyer indicated it is technically not my responsibility to handle her affairs. And with that, in January of 2013, Mom headed back to Maryland. The year of 2013 became a blur as I was in Florida and observed the struggle between my two sisters continue from afar. Of course being updated by one or the other sister by phone call. The pressure, court hearings, mishandling of money, and pure will of Rebecca to get Tina removed would eventually come to fruition. Tina expressed her desire to vacate the position. In December of 2013, due to these circumstances, I had to make the tough decision to petition the court for the removal of Tina. This would now be the second petition of removal as Rebecca already filed one back in July of 2012.

05

Family Heartbreak

In 2014, the need for proper care of Mom was becoming urgent. Her dementia progressed and her affairs were mishandled. But the court needed proof that Mom was in a situation not suitable for her. And so the court's assigned ad litem and a care assessment manager evaluated Mom at Tina's home while under her care.[8] Whenever Mom's guardianship changed, this process had to happen. Mom's mental and physical capacities were evaluated and reported.

The court found that Tina's townhome was exactly the same as Mom's residence that was deemed unsafe for someone with limited physical abilities. Meaning the layout with multiple stories and narrow stairways was not proper for Mom to live in daily. The care assessment manager reported that Mom was somewhat unsteady on her feet, although she did not use a cane or walker. She was able to ambulate down the stairs but only with close stand-by assistance. They also reported that Mom was missing several doctor appointments. Although I had my suspicions of Rebecca's previous complaints, when the pharmacy started calling my house in Florida to pick up medicine in Maryland, I knew I had to step in.

Together, my sister Rebecca and I decided to share in Mom's care and petitioned the court to appoint us the responsibility of co-guardians.[9] Our legal responsibilities began in February 2014. At that court hearing, all parties agreed and interpreted in good faith that Rebecca would complete the needed renovations to Mom's home to accommodate a dementia patient. It was also understood that Rebecca would receive reimbursement from the sale of the home after Mom's passing and the estate settled.

Additionally, the court order allowed Mom to remain in Virginia with Rebecca with specific instructions that Mom be delivered by March 2014 into my physical care until the renovations were completed at her home in Alexandria. In compliance with the court order, Rebecca returned Mom to me in Florida.

Early April 2014, one month later, is when I received a phone call from Rebecca requesting that Mom travel with her back to Virginia for a mini vacation. Considering that Mom was well into her 90s, Rebecca mentioned that this may be her last trip to Virginia and her birthplace, Riner. I agreed to the trip with a promise to return Mom back to Florida for a follow-up doctor's appointment scheduled in July 2014.[10] Since we were co-guardians and had a doctor's permission, Mom returned to Virginia with Rebecca. And this is when I first felt the sting of betrayal directed at me.

Learning of the Marriage

One Saturday morning in June 2014, while attending my grandson's basketball game, my phone rang. I received the most alarming and shocking news of my lifetime. My uncle informed me that Mom, who has had dementia for three years at this point, is walking down the aisle. He was stunned to hear that his sister was literally at a church exchanging wedding vows with her "friend," Eddie. Unbelievably overwhelmed by this news, his first thought was to call and inform me. We learned later that the marriage license, without our knowledge, had already been issued a month prior to the ceremony. In short, while Mom was on a planned vacation to Virginia (April 2014 thru July 2014), she fell victim to a plotted arranged marriage. I immediately placed a call to the minister to inform him that Mom had been declared an incapacitated adult in 2011. At that point, Mom was unable to handle any of her business affairs or activities.

In the days ahead, steps were taken to verify the change made in Mom's marital status. It was a far-fetched idea that my sister, as Mom's co-guardian, would allow such a thing. Once verified through court records that a license had been obtained, I had no choice but to challenge the validity of the marriage. Mom, who was diagnosed with moderate dementia, should not have been legally qualified to sign a license to marry. But, in questioning the marriage, I found that the license had been obtained in an adjacent county where Mom was not registered as legally incapacitated. Therefore, because Mom was able to physically sign her name, the court excused themselves from this matter. More trickery from Rebecca.

It's Not Okay

Rebecca, with this idea of marrying Mom and Eddie, knew the news outlets and media would fall in love over a story like this one. She took them to any news outlet willing to listen. We even heard Rebecca was pursuing Guinness World Records to promote the story. To be honest, I do not believe she knew it would explode to this extent. It was like she threw a dart blindly, and it just so happened to hit the bullseye. The perfect storm, so to speak. Who would even think that so many people would pay attention to our little family? But here we are.

At this point, I do not know how my home phone still functions after the number of calls I was receiving. It felt like my entire family and friends back home in Maryland and Virginia asked if I saw the news publication. I pulled up a web browser, typed my mother's name and BOOM, every link on the search page had the story. Even seeing this with my very own eyes, still did not register to me the amount of traction this story was receiving. As each news station highlighted and reported a love story, I watched in disbelief and disappointment. I made an attempt to inform the news media that the love story contained many inaccuracies. My attempts to tell the other side of the story were totally ignored. Every station in the DMV region continued to push the story.

It became very clear that Mom's return to Florida as promised by my sister was not going to happen. Unfortunately, Mom's scheduled appointment with the oncologist had to be cancelled. I then petitioned the court for a hearing requesting a replacement for my sister Rebecca considering the irresponsible activity that had occurred.[11]

Once again, in August 2014, I found myself in the same fifth circuit court in Alexandria standing in front of the same judge who had previously declared Mom incapacitated three years earlier. The judge, having dealt with our family on multiple occasions and witnessing the back and forth between all the different siblings, decided to vacate the positions. This led to the assignment of an independent third-party guardian, Jessica Niesen. Rebecca would challenge the decision instantly in court by telling the judge "I'll be back."

The outcome of the decision made by the court to remove us as guardians enabled the story to look like a sister feud to the public. Mom's life was now in total chaos. Jessica Niesen, her new guardian, immediately began doing her job to restore order. She reached out to me and my sisters via phone call or letter. Little did she know at the time what the court signed her up for. The crosshairs lie squarely on Jessica now.

Under visitation rights, Mom would remain in Virginia with Rebecca. Because Mom was still under Rebecca's care, Jessica could hardly reach her. Once again, ignoring phone calls and efforts to reach out after many failed attempts, Jessica requested and secured a conference meeting with Rebecca and Mom. There was only one problem, a huge problem, Rebecca showed up to Jessica's office alone without Mom. The meeting ended with Rebecca spewing the words, "Her husband Eddie is the guardian now." As if anybody outside of the court could make that decision. The court decides when to relinquish guardianship, Rebecca had no authority to make such a decision in an attempt to override the court decision already in place.

Although Rebecca was causing more drama, I was willing to talk and communicate with Jessica. We arranged a meeting in Virginia. I flew up with every intention to iron out the future plans for our mother.

"In a perfect world," Jessica asked me, "what would you want for your mom?"

I responded, "To live out the rest of her life safe and comfortable."

My family and Jessica discussed the decision to annul the marriage given the irresponsible nature of it all. Under Jessica's guidance, with compassion for the elders, and since Mom was in fact a friend of Eddie, a decision was made to keep the friendship together. Initially believing that keeping them local in Virginia was the best idea: Tina, Jessica, Uncle Hubbard (Mom's brother), and I were looking for housing accommodations for them. Their combined income was limited and insufficient, which made it nearly impossible for suitable placement. The elders were incapable of living independently without assistance.[12] Rebecca stated in one of her many interviews, "Let them be happy." This was the perfect opportunity for Rebecca to care for the couple in her home in Annandale, Virginia.

While in Rebecca's care, many family members expressed concern over their inability to visit Mom, never knowing where to find her. Even Eddie's nephew was looking for him in search of rent payment. The family complaints would grow louder as they also were unable to speak with Mom. My Uncle Hubbard was unable to make contact with his sister on many occasions. When Uncle Hubbard eventually made any interaction, he was alarmed to see his sister had suffered major weight loss.[18] He voiced his concern to me and Tina. This is when we began receiving reports that Rebecca was in the process of filming Mom and Eddie in numerous locations.

With numerous complaints about Rebecca being directed to Jessica from family members, I asked if Mom could come to Florida for a visit while we figure out the next steps. Being legally bound to take care of Mom, Jessica honored my request.[13] The mishandling of medication, Mom's weight loss, and having both elders in unsafe environments were all factors which also influenced Jessica to search for a stable situation. In this particular circumstance, and in combination with Eddie's reluctance, Jessica had no legal ties over Eddie to help him. Rebecca was his power of attorney.

The original agreement was for me to pick Mom up at her house. I recommended to Jessica that the exchange should happen in a public place, like a police station, based off prior events involving Rebecca. It was supposed to be my husband Rayfield, Uncle Hubbard, Lois, Tina, Rebecca, Mom, and me present during the exchange. The final agreed upon location was a restaurant. Tina did not show up. Jessica was not present. While Uncle Hubbard was already in route for the transfer, he was called by Rebecca and told not to come. Knowing what I know now, this move had to be a calculated action. If Uncle Hubbard were to show up, the storyline would be ruined. Rebecca and Laura Checkoway would not have been able to create the false visual that portrays Jessica, my husband, and me as villains with my uncle present.

The Unfiltered Truth

December 6th, 2014, the day of transfer, Rebecca and Mom were a no-show at the agreed location. My husband, Lois, and I, along with two great grandchildren waited over an hour at the All-American Steak house on US 1 in Alexandria to make the exchange. I finally placed a call to Jessica for further instructions. I was told to swing by Mom's home, and she would meet me there. And with that the scene was set. On the cloudy evening, I proceeded to Mom's home as instructed.

Lights, Camera, Action!

Film crew outside of Mom's Home waiting for us to arrive.

Rain, doom, and gloom. It felt like everything was set up perfectly for dramatics. We arrived, cars were parked up and down the street. There were camera crews across the street and on the sidewalks. I noticed a few of the cars had New York tags. I was ambushed as I approached the house. The paparazzi would be proud of this crew the way they were running across the street to capture any piece of footage they could.

More cameras were positioned directly outside the house, on the first floor, and on the stairs leading to the second floor where Mom's bedroom was. The house was filled with guests. Without any paperwork, and being met with resistance from Rebecca, I walked back outside to call the police and wait for Jessica. I wanted to avoid any altercations to make this process as smooth as possible. When the police arrived, they asked preliminary questions regarding the situation. When Jessica appeared with legal documents, the police moved forward with clearing the house.

My husband took one step upstairs, and Rebecca was already acting like a seasoned Oscar-nominated actress. Lights, cameras, and Rebecca were all pointing in his direction. She was screaming like the main character of a scary movie. It's no wonder they did not want to meet at the restaurant. He gazed at the camera with one thing to say, "If I appear in any footage, I will sue everybody in here." And that was that.

The camera crew was certainly ready to take advantage, especially upstairs in Mom's bedroom. I walked in, it looked prepared for a movie premiere. The elders had been placed in bed side by side, fully clothed. One man had a camera so enormous he had to hold it up on his shoulders. The room was barely big enough to fit a bed and dresser, let alone have all these people in it. Police, film crew, and family members bunched in a small room was a very uncomfortable feeling.

I wanted to ask Mom, "When did you get a new home entertainment system?" The way they had audio equipment and hidden mics set up all over surely resembled one. While the commotion upstairs proceeded, I noticed Rebecca went downstairs. I followed her to the kitchen where I overheard her speaking with a lawyer. This was confirmation that someone famous was involved in our family affairs. It was discovered that the lawyer speaking with Rebecca was connected to an A-list celebrity. Even though I knew they were up to something, I had no idea how far their antics would go.

So, as history has proved, giving Rebecca an inch means she will take a mile. With no real contest to the marriage, the narrative of a true love story would play out to much of the family's dismay. Most of the Edith + Eddie documentary was created after this point, between April 2014 and December 2014. All of our lives as we knew it would change forever. The saga begins.

06

Hearts Are Red

The day after the transfer. We make it back to Florida before the crack of dawn, about 3:00 a.m. Rebecca was already on the phone calling a few hours later, and when she did not get a response she immediately called her lawyer claiming that we were ignoring her. This is the same person who would go weeks without calling to let close family know the status or whereabouts of Mom. Because of the fiasco at Mom's house, we were forced to take the last flight of the evening.

Not looking to cause anymore unnecessary strain, Mom and Eddie were able to communicate that same day. Mom let him know that she was fine.

In the ensuing weeks, Mom and Eddie talked on the phone periodically. Mom was content with the two-minute communications they had. She never expressed a desire to go back home to Virginia. Eddie's physical condition had been noticeably deteriorating for some time. He chose not to come to Florida for the visit. He appeared sickly just as Mom did. On Eddie's behalf, APS was called. We were notified a short time later that Eddie was hospitalized. I told Mom of the circumstances, she replied "Poor boy, did his people go see about him?"

Rebecca, with access to an A-list celebrity's attorney, demanded that Mom return to say her final goodbye to Eddie. Mom was in no condition to travel again in this short span. Rebecca had no respect for Mom's health conditions and certainly did not care how that may affect her under these circumstances. Her care assessment manager stated in a letter that, due to frailness, weakness, and problems with mental recall it would not be a recommended trip.[14] Although APS was notified that Eddie was in need of assistance, he unfortunately succumbed to his illnesses. Eddie officially passed away in December of 2014.[16]

In February of 2015, Mom's care assessment manager from Virginia was sent to evaluate and analyze my home. Pictures were taken of various living spaces within my house to report the findings and conditions. I completed a Medicare examination which included her contentment level.[17] There was also a one-on-one private interview conducted. In court records, concerning my husband, Mom's response to a question was "Oh, Pat's husband. Oh yes, he is very nice."[19]

There were allegations of abuse by Rebecca made against my husband while we were picking up my mother. In front of a film crew was the first time we heard such a thing. If those allegations were true and really occurred, you would think my sister would have alerted the family or the court to protect our mother. She did not; it never happened. I believe Rebecca rehearsed the abuse claims until Mom repeated them. One of the most unbelievable things to hear. I suddenly had flashbacks of the warning Lewis gave me. Rebecca made these same claims of abuse about Lewis and others within the family.

March of 2015, and more legal issues surface. Rebecca has petitioned the court.[20] The hidden motive for doing so centered around the documentary being created. Under the mask of holding Jessica accountable to her words, Rebecca's ulterior motive was to continue filming Mom. Any time Rebecca had a dispute, court fees were charged against Mom's estate.[21] Instead of battling Jessica, I was in constant communication, sending reports on Mom's wellbeing. It had been several years since Mom could hold a comprehensive conversation, but Jessica was in contact whenever possible.

Insert Cher, the TV and musical icon, who witnessed the story through a news clip. In court, Cher gave a virtual deposition. Under the impression that Mom and Eddie were a long-standing couple and looking to do the right thing, under oath, she offered to renovate the home. Somehow Cher was told, or under the notion, that I wanted Mom in a nursing home. Unfortunately, she had received misinformation and believed it.

The judge wanted to make everyone happy. He decided to allow Mom to remain in Florida. Mom was to remain until the renovations to her home were complete. Cher wanted to show her compassion and generosity. She committed to setting up a trust to facilitate the transformation of Mom's home. The judge also put forth orders to end all filming of our mother.

Estimates for the renovations were to be sent to Cher. As a condition of Mom's return to her home, promptly upon the acceptance of the estimates, the benefactor (Cher) was supposed to pay the necessary funds into a trust account maintained by Jessica. The condition was that there needed to be enough money for the renovation and one full year of expenses for care costs. Because the care assessment manager determined Mom's best interest was not under Rebecca's care, Cher would have to pay for a third party 24/7 service to look after Mom. Those cost estimates reached ranges upward of $180,000 for the year.[21] This was on top of the $50,000 renovation budget to install a wheel chair ramp and organize all essential living quarters to be on the same floor. With these estimations in place, Cher suddenly disappeared for unknown reasons.

Mom's Vacation

Mom had no idea all this conflict was happening, her life in Florida was relatively simple. She regained the lost weight and continuously claimed she was living the "Life of Riley." She described her new living environment as paradise. Mom received lots of attention wherever we would go. She befriended the ladies at the hair salon and loved the special attention given to her.

Mom also enjoyed going to doctor appointments for the same reasons. Arrangements were made for her to attend an adult daycare center where she would enjoy lunch and engage in appropriate activities. The beaches and view of the ocean always pleased her as she would say, "This is God's world, he just lets us live in it."

Mom enjoyed her great grandson (Patrick), and visits from her older great grandson (Keith), always telling him how good looking he is. Patrick at eight years old was a real pleasure for her to watch as he completed his homework and read stories to her. She would always say, "he is going to be somebody important." She often looked forward to attending Mt. Calvary Church each Sunday, she would sing along with the hymns and enjoyed the sermons. Mom would sing, "Oh how I love Jesus, because he first loved me" and "Oh when the saints go marching in," with a hired assistant.

My sister Tina would communicate with Mom over the phone often. I was able to coordinate Mom's availability to anybody who wanted to speak with her. Tina insisted on needing her own vacation, so we scheduled a visit for her to come down to Florida. When Tina arrived we planned a dinner at a local diner. It was an "all you can eat" restaurant. We sat down to enjoy our first round of food. When Tina got up to get more food, our mother asked, "who is that lady?" I had to remind Mom that her oldest daughter was in town for a visit. When Tina came back to her seat and attempted to engage in conversation, she shockingly realized Mom no longer knew who she was by appearance. She only knew of her daughter by name. Having witnessed this experience with her own eyes, Tina returned home understanding the severity of mom's mental condition.

After Tina left, Rebecca attempted to arrange an emergency visit for herself. She contacted lawyers who reached out to the guardian Jessica to schedule a visit. Apparently Tina told Rebecca the story, because all of a sudden Rebecca requested a meeting in a hotel with a neurologist present. Evidently, Rebecca wanted to be in "fake denial" about the condition of Mom with such a ridiculous request. She used the excuse of bringing a neurologist to attempt to control the situation. What real information about Mom's health would be discovered in a hotel room. Previous Doctors and other healthcare professionals ran actual lab tests and procedures, which all lead to the same sentiments. Once the onset of dementia has occurred, the disease can progress rapidly as time goes on.

Although there were no neurologist nor hotel rooms, there was an open invitation at the adult daycare center Mom attended. We scheduled a visit for Rebecca to meet with Mom on a specific day. It was cleared through the director of the facility. The staff were prepared and ready for the visit between 12 p.m. and 4 p.m. When I went to pick up Mom from the facility, I was told there were no visitors who showed up.

We would receive cards in the mail from Rebecca constantly. Anywhere from once a week to twice a week. I started wondering why Rebecca was sending cards knowing our mother could no longer read, instead of just visiting our mother in person. Rebecca never visited Mom for the entire time she was in Florida. Nonetheless, we took turns reading the cards to Mom. One day a card was sent with a plastic sleeve and book marker. There was a white powdery substance in the package. I do not know if it was salt, sugar, sand, or something worse. But I was reluctant to open it. It immediately reminded me of the Anthrax era, a very serious situation.

Come to find out this card was signed by Rebecca and Dr. Buzzard. Because I had never heard of a Dr. Buzzard in or around our family, I looked him up, called a few friends from Virginia, and realized this card was "with love" from a well-known Voodoo doctor in Alexandria Virginia. I am under the impression that the first few letters were a set up to the other mysterious ones. Some of these letters had an animal reference for seemingly other family member's names.

One day Rebecca called to speak to mom. My husband happened to answer the phone this time around. We've grown accustomed to automatically turning the speaker on whenever we knew she was reaching out. This was so we had two minds to interpret or decipher any antics Rebecca would pull to be manipulative. On que, our intuition came to fruition, Rebecca demanded to speak to mom. My husband told her that Mom was sleeping. Rebecca said, "I don't believe you." His response was "Ask Dr. Buzzard!" Rebecca proceeded to rant about him opening and reading her mail.

We received guidance from our home care providers for certain situations, which Rebecca completely disregarded. The instruction was not to disturb Mom during sleep for phone calls. I called to let Rebecca know the best time to reach Mom was right after dinner around 7p.m. Not only did Rebecca refuse to call around that time, most of the time, there would also be odd instances where someone called between 2 a.m. and 3 a.m. from an unknown number. To this day we do not know if she was trying to Voodoo one person, our mother, or the whole family. After these incidents, we decided if any more of these letters were to be opened, it had to be across the street and out the house.

The curiosity of my grandson Keith got the best of him, he decided to retrieve the cards Rebecca sent to the house that were left in the shed. He wanted to see and read them. To my disbelief, my husband actually left them outside of the shed. Each card was entangled and merged together. After all those years, enduring the various nature elements, here is the remainder of them.

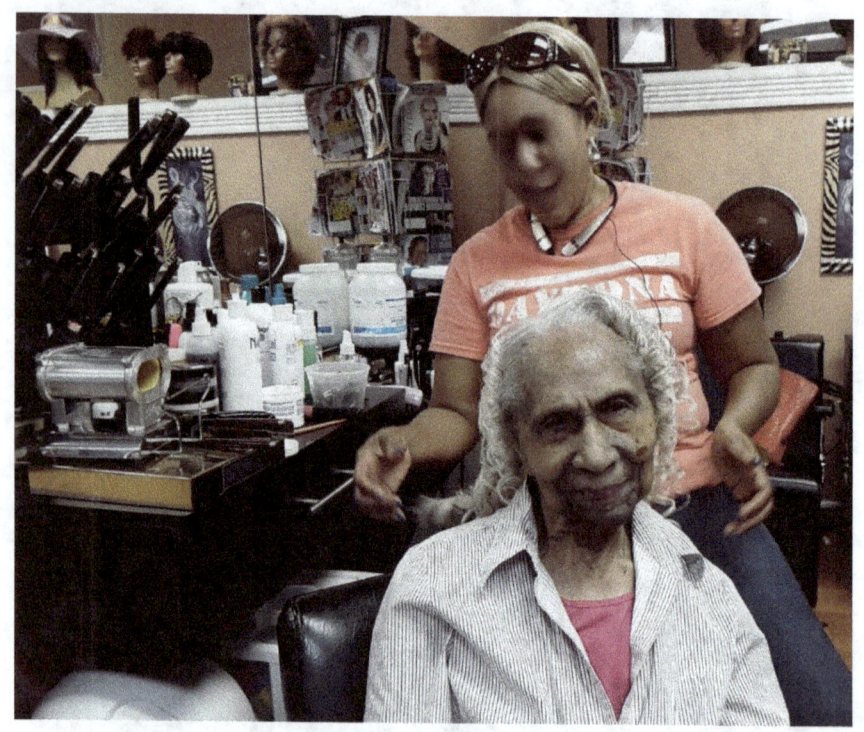

Mom (singing): "When I take my vacation in heaven, will you take your vacation with me. Sitting down on the banks of the river, beneath the shade of an evergreen tree."

Hairdresser (laughing): "I think you should let him take that vacation without you."

This song was in reference to her first boyfriend in Piney woods who played the guitar. He used to sing this song to her. She often bragged about being a country girl who lived deep in the woods. She spent the rest of her life singing this song anywhere and to anybody, even while at the hairdresser's. It is the very same song you hear her sing at the end of the documentary.

As the years and months went by, Rebecca never visited her mother in Florida. Robin, my sister's daughter, followed the actions of her mother by never visiting. It seems they no longer had any concerns about the abuse they claimed was going on in my household, nor did they care about the health conditions Mom was enduring. Rebecca has a residence in Florida. Both of them were accustomed to traveling, frequently making the long trip between Virginia and Florida. These types of actions left me suspicious about their level of sincerity.

March 21st, 2017, started off as a regular morning. I opened the curtains and let the sun shine through. Mom and I were getting ready for one of her doctor appointments, which she always enjoyed. I prepared her oatmeal, so she had something on her stomach. Mom needed to go to the bathroom one last time before we left. I stood in the doorway and waited patiently. I glanced over, Mom's head suddenly dropped, I then lifted her head up to see if she was ok. Noticed her shoulders dropped also, and she slumped. As chills rushed down my spine, hands sweating profusely, there was no time for fear. I laid her on the floor in the bathroom and yelled for my husband to call 911. I placed a damp cloth on her forehead. After I lifted her legs, we placed a pillow under her head and removed her teeth so she would not choke.

EMTs arrived within seven minutes, they rushed straight to the bathroom. Amidst the commotion, "Does she have a DNR (Do Not Resuscitate order)?" they asked. I responded that she did not have one and answered all their questions about her medications. They loaded Mom into the ambulance and worked on her for what felt like an eternity. Eventually, they decide to transport her to the hospital. When we arrived, the staff escorted us to a private room and delivered the news. The Doctor said, "what a way to go," because she passed away from natural causes. Our mom, Edith Hill, had transitioned to the other side at the age of ninety-eight, just a few months shy of her ninety-ninth birthday.

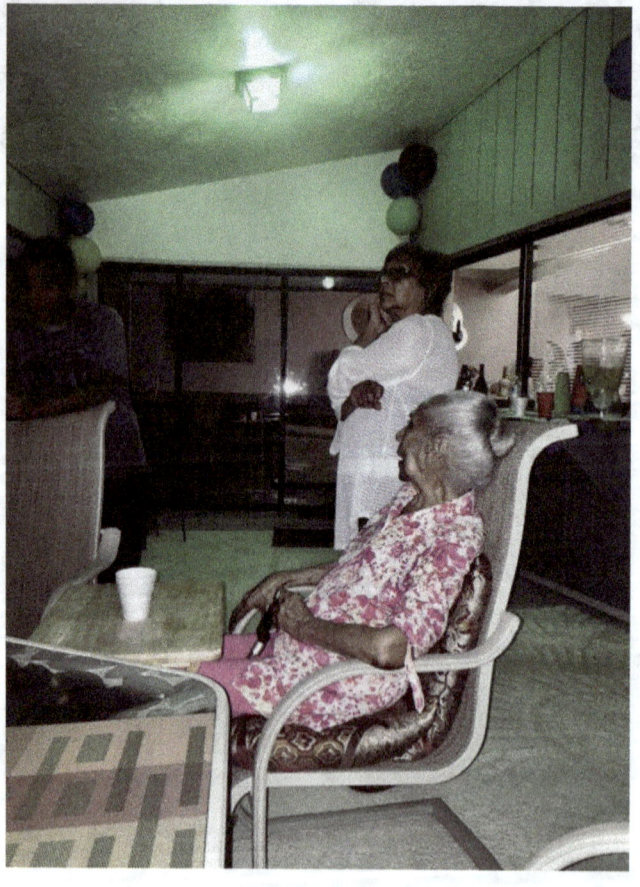

07

Blood Is Blue

If you thought Mom's passing was the end of this story, it was a new beginning. You see, this is the same time the world gets introduced to Edith + Eddie. I had already endured some legal struggles involving my sister. Already saved my mother from the circus of an environment Rebecca had her in. And already taken care of my mother for over two years. There was no mention of these subsequent two years and four months of care at my home.

I wanted to have the funeral in Virginia where most of our family members resided. After Mom was embalmed in Florida, we could not release the body to leave the state due to the confusion surrounding her formal name. Is her last name Hill or Harrison? Hill being the last name she had ever since her last husband passed away, and Harrison being Eddie's last name. The funeral home would not allow Mom to be moved until her name was validated. The guardian reached out to the mortuary, and Mom's name was cleared.

Due to the mishap, Mom's original flight from Orlando to Dulles could not happen. Ironically, once things were settled, Mom, my husband and I flew back to Virginia on the same flight out of Jacksonville. So Edith Hill, her official name, was how she took her last flight accompanying me and my husband. Although she did not have a seat next to me, looking out into the clouds, I knew her spirit was guiding me. I protected her, and now she's a guardian angel protecting me. Countless family and friends converged on Alexandria, to celebrate the life of Mom. Besides the sorrow of losing a loved one, everyone took the moment to reminisce about the good times. Seeing family for the first time in a very long time was a good feeling. The support I received was overwhelming.

Even though everyone was there to say their final goodbyes, I could not help but notice a couple of people who were missing. Rebecca, my sister, the one who caused this whole fiasco, was not in attendance. Neither was her daughter, Robin. My mom's brother, my uncle Hubbard, communicated that Rebecca made a threatening phone call to disrupt the service and expose the family. The minster had multiple law enforcement officers present due to that threat. I was very disappointed that Rebecca and her daughter did not attend Mom's celebration of life.

It felt like the directors strategically waited for her to pass away to release the documentary. After further research, we discovered the film was released a couple weeks prior to Mom's passing in the same month. I thought back on Rebecca's actions also. It felt as if she was just waiting, and only checking on Mom to see if and when she passed away. Nothing felt sincere and not showing up to the funeral confirmed it.

Tina (Sister) and Me at Mom's funeral.

Uncle Hubbard, me, and family.

A Night at the Movies

(A Letter from Rayfield)

There was a mandatory business meeting I needed to attend in Chicago. I coordinated my travel plans to spend a couple days in town. While I was there I received a call from my wife. She just spoke with a family member who was concerned about a movie going around. She reminded me of all the rumored filming her sister was doing a few months ago, and that a film was completed. I was stunned to find out a motion picture actually came to fruition, and that this story is circulating about her family nationwide.

We searched and found out many shows were available. The internet was buzzing with information concerning the festival viewings. One that stood out immediately was The Chicago International Film Festival. Since I was already there to handle my responsibilities, I decided to extend my stay so I could attend.

It was a Sunday in October of 2017. The festival ran from October 12th until October 26th. I drove to downtown Chicago to figure out what was going on. The documentary was shown at a movie complex that had multiple levels. When I had to take an escalator to get to the theatre, I knew this was not going to be some mom-and-pop movie. If they did enough to make it here, this very well may be a feature film. As the stairs continued to elevate, I suddenly became anxious. Up until this point, we had no idea what was being said in the film.

As I entered, they handed out cards to personally critique the different films for Q&A. It's finally here, the film I have been waiting on. As the scenes were moving along, it did not take very long to realize this film was going to get ugly. Rebecca threw some accusations against my wife that were not true.

About half way through the movie, I could not believe my ears. Not only did Rebecca take shots at my wife, she threw me under the bus. Taken aback, my eyes were wide open. You would have thought someone just smacked my face the way my cheeks and eyes bubbled up. Within seconds I felt lightheaded. Like a punch to the chest, suffocating could describe the grasp for air I took. I looked around the theatre nervously. I did not know if my face would appear in this film. Thoughts running wild, I had a flashback.

I've known Rebecca for over sixty years, I seriously thought we had a brother/sister type of relationship. Our families have known each other for an even longer period of time. Rebecca is the one who initially introduced me to her sister Patricia back in high school. There was a twenty-five-year period where we went our separate ways. Life happened, but Rebecca kept the line of communication open as she would visit my parents in Virginia often. Eventually, I was reintroduced to Patricia, and guess who made that connection happen: Rebecca. I finally snapped out of the mini dream I had. Felt like I had an out-of-body experience, thinking someone was going to come out and say this is all a joke. But that never happened, I was in a nightmare situation.

I left early because everything was running long, and I needed to catch a late flight back to Florida. The Q&A for Edith + Eddie started later. Looking back, it may have been a good thing as I would have stood up and told the whole theatre who I was. Not knowing what the reaction of the audience may have been, whether they would have given me a round of applause for standing up for myself, or chased me out of that theatre not knowing the depth of the situation. There is another side of this story, the real side of this story. I headed for the exit and never looked back. I flew back to Florida with a story to tell my wife.

08
Circulation

The documentary began moving across the world, let alone the country. Imagine being blindsided by a film where your character is in question. The worst part is that your own sister is the ring leader doing most of the bashing. Festival after festival, the motion picture gained tremendous steam as it vilified me, Jessica, and my husband.

I called my sons and grown grandson over to watch the movie. I am now hearing all the statements being made in the film. All the hard work that goes into taking care of another life was thrown aside for vulgar and misleading comments. I began to process all the actions that were taken by Rebecca and the film crew in order to create this documentary. And it is starting to make sense, even though it does not make any sense why my sister would stoop to this level. And why the directors never bothered to interview Mom's other two daughters before producing the film. If a documentary is made under the assumption that the contents within are true, the morally correct thing to do is explore the other side of the story for validity, which never happened. The director never attempted to communicate with me.

After watching the film in its entirety, my grandson, Keith, immediately reviewed the comments being made on social media. We all witnessed the nasty and explosive opinions of people viewing the documentary from a filtered point of view. I found the documentary deeply disturbing to watch because of the many lies and edited film clips including the many prompts.

Safety became a concern for Jessica, me, and my family. Hateful posts and threats spread across the internet like wildfire. Within a few weeks, security cameras were installed around my home due to the amount of people inciting violence as their next course of action. A blind eye had been turned to benefit others.

Insert Laura Checkoway, the director and producer. I now know the name and face behind the documentary. An article interviewing her asks questions surrounding the tall tale she influenced. She states that a friend texted her a photo of the "couple," after seeing it on the news, and that is how she became interested in the story.

A reviewer, Glenn Dunks of Archive Junkee, made a statement: he said, **"I just wish director Laura Checkoway had confronted any of the issues that her documentary raises."** By the time you finish reading this book, you will know exactly why she chose not to confront said issues. The threat that this story may not be 100% true is surely a reason not to pursue the other side. It just is not as interesting. From their perspective, a story of this caliber would surely bolster a career. A now Oscar-nominated career. It was vital for the narrative to remain a "dramatic love story," and not engaging the other sisters or family members ensured that. So both the directors and Rebecca needed to document the story the same way. Again, the perfect storm of events.

Cher, the Goddess of Pop, having inserted herself in the middle of this twisted tale, conveniently reappears. Having helped push this documentary to its height of Oscar and Emmy nominations, Cher's involvement was instrumental in the film going mainstream. She and Laura Checkoway went on many interviews surrounding the story. I do not know the dynamics of their relationship. But one day searching the internet I viewed a photo of the two of them sitting together on a sofa and, at some point, Cher became engulfed in this documentary as the executive producer. A major blow to the side of truth. It went from Cher potentially helping a sensitive situation to me standing up to a powerful figure as an "adversary." The uphill battle begins.

Since the singer decided to voice her opinion, a factually wrong opinion, I now have to defend myself. In court, Cher said that I wanted to put my mother in a facility, which is factually incorrect. I wanted to put my mother in the most suitable living arrangement.

According to The Hollywood Reporter, Cher says ***"I was going to have to retrofit their house so that they could stay there, which really was making some repairs and putting a full bathroom downstairs. Then things started to change. All of a sudden, they had to renovate the entire house. It was now up in the hundreds of thousands of dollars."***

Well, from this quote it sounds like she understands the severity of the situation. Any house "needing" hundreds of thousands of dollars to fix sounds unsafe. We need to be more specific though. This house, built in 1947, had less than 900 square feet of living space, a leaky roof, electrical issues, lead pipes, rodents, and steep twisting stairs. Not to mention it was three stories tall, with the laundry machines down in the unfinished basement.

In the same quote she proceeds to say, ***"And then, while we're trying to figure this out, one night, Hill's guardian comes with the police and drags her out of the house."***

We did not have time to go back and forth in court on whether Cher would shell out any money to renovate the house. Nor were we really looking for any money. She was no real factor in our family's efforts to care for our mom. Either she will help or not. But Edith and Eddie were literally in the middle of a dangerous situation.

The Hollywood Reporter asked her about personal significance and how she feels about a film being made. She states, *"They were not treated like people. They weren't treated with the respect that age demands."*

Cher actually never met Mom or Eddie to know the scope of how they were treated by me. I did not appreciate her making such an accusation. Had she done the proper research, the fairy godmother would have realized who was actually treating them inhumanely. And that she was on the wrong side of this situation.

Cher tells the story of her grandfather being put in a home. They quoted her as saying, *"I went to visit him, and I saw all these people just warehoused in this place. My grandfather didn't speak the whole time I was there. I turned to him and said: 'I am getting you out of here. I don't care what anyone says.' And the only thing he said to me the whole time I was there was, 'Don't delay.' I got him out of there."*

After reading these quotes from her, I am wondering why I could not do the same. I went to save my mother and I do not care what anyone says. Any care that our mother needed was provided solely by my husband and me. Had Cher cared for the other side of the story, these reckless comments may not exist. The facts: she did not help after spewing all these quotes in the media. The trust account for the renovations of the home and care for my mother was never funded by Cher. Once again, Cher never met Mom or Eddie.

Truth of the matter, my home in Florida is considered elderly friendly, including proper accessories to care for a dementia patient in their nineties such as handrails in the bathroom. I live in a one-story home that is wheelchair accessible. The warmth of the sunshine state proved to be very suitable for Mom. The blistering, bone crushing winters in the north are a tough place for anyone to live especially as you age. This is one of the many reasons elders decide to retire to Florida.

09

Breathe Without Air

In twenty-nine minutes, Edith + Eddie, the 2018 Oscar- and Emmy-nominated documentary was crafted to evoke your anger and your sympathy, while filling you with questions and disbelief. The truth matters. This professionally edited film is presented as a touching romantic story of two elderly people in love and their melodramatic, seemingly tragic, separation. The elders had been coached to believe outrageous lies, instilled with fear of losing Mom's home and a permanent separation. There are verifiable court records made available to the public in the 5th circuit court in Alexandria, Virginia which dispel the notion of any of the wrongdoing portrayed in the film.

It is not ok to turn a blind eye or ignore elders with apparent disabilities who also show visual and mental incapacitations. It is not ok to intrude into the lives of seniors and adversely affect their lives. Whether through social networks, media exposure, or other forms of public attention, using their image, stories, or private moments for personal or financial gain violates their dignity and privacy. Seniors deserve respect, protection, and the freedom to live without the added burden of unwanted interference or exploitation by others seeking recognition, profit, or influence. Edith + Eddie not only misrepresents the elders, it overlooks and grossly misrepresents Jessica, my husband, and me. The proposed evil villains portrayed in the film were actually the protectors of the defenseless elders.

Mom's friend Eddie resided in Alexandria and rented from his nephew through the entire friendship with her. Mom and Eddie never lived together.

Mom's house, located near the Pentagon, and situated within Oldtown Alexandria was rich with history. It was worth half a million dollars at the time, a far cry from what she actually had in her possession. Mom never knew how "rich" she was. Based on her income at the time, the home would have been sold to pay for care at a facility. Many facilities in the area wanted north of $6,000 a month to provide care. The 500-thousand-dollar price tag is more than enough motivation for a greedy family member to want it all, and go to extremes to get it.

Gifted Liar

Rebecca was very stealthy, and yet loud, with what she was looking to accomplish. Family members are coming forward expressing that she planned to secure Mom's house years ago. There was no indication that she intended to share any of the proceeds with her siblings. Rebecca went from household to household spreading stories.

Over time, she acquired numerous items, including cars, computers, houses, and money. People experiencing unfortunate situations, the elderly, the incapacitated, the sickly, and even ones on their death bed were all open season for Rebecca. It was hard for family members to fathom that she would stoop so low. The puzzle pieces were always fuzzy and not completely in order, but to attempt to obtain her mother's house may have topped them all.

The documentary featured select family members. Only her daughter, Robin, and Mom's aging sister fell in line with the unethical master plan to achieve Rebecca's goal. This situation finally sparked a bright light in our family's minds: Rebecca had been the source of many rumors, lies, and scandals over the years.

I ask you to focus on these facts:

1. Eddie's family was in no way involved, even at his passing.
2. A documentary of this magnitude had only three blood relatives of Mom involved.
3. The "marriage" happened secretly, but was made a public spectacle after the fact.

When I questioned Rebecca about the marriage, she said, "It was a private matter." The more you know, the more apparent the hidden agenda becomes. We now know that Rebecca became Eddie's power of attorney just before the arranged marriage or shortly thereafter. By doing so, Rebecca would attempt to control both of their assets.

There is nothing wrong with accepting an inheritance; that is part of society's social construct. That is the goal of many parents, to pass down the love and wealth that hopefully gives the next generation a head start. The problem arises when one sibling wants it all. I noticed a plot unfolding and intervened. If not for my actions, Rebecca would have carried out her plans, potentially leaving all the other siblings with no inheritance at all. I acted to carry out the wishes that Mom had been sharing with us for years.

Mom had a Will in place. Rebecca was able to amend it, but she left in the fact that Mom indeed wanted me to be the Executor in Uncle Hubbard's absence.[22]

Exploitation of Eddie

I want to take a moment to describe some of the ways in which Eddie was taken advantage of in this whole story. Interviews of family members uncovered some disturbing information. Eddie was exhibiting signs of poor health and a need for around-the-clock healthcare while under the supervision of Rebecca. The documentary is not the first time Eddie was admitted to a hospital while with Rebecca. According to family testimonies, on a trip to Christiansburg, Eddie fell ill and landed in a local emergency room after he was fed buffalo meat.

With these types of experiences, Eddie's relationship with Rebecca grew, based on a perceived notion that she was taking care of him. Without any guidance, he ultimately gave her permission to be his power of attorney. He did not understand the consequences of his actions. After a phone call from Eddie's nephew, we discovered that Eddie's money had been removed and his bank account was completely depleted.[15] Only Eddie and Rebecca's names were on that account.

Rebecca was made aware that the time had come to remove Eddie from life support and he would soon pass. As Eddie lay in the hospital bed as viewed in the documentary, his life savings were withdrawn from his bank account, just days prior to him being taken off life support. He was stripped of his funeral funds. According to Eddie's nephew, that money was reserved for his funeral plans. When Rebecca was questioned about the empty bank account in court, she claimed Eddie took a loan out from her "friend" in Florida.

Even after his passing, Eddie remained in the hospital morgue for several weeks. Instead of covering his funeral expenses, after crying at his bedside for a documentary and with his missing money, Rebecca informed Jessica that Eddie had a wife. Nevertheless, Mom's funds initially paid for Eddie's cremation. Eventually, his retirement plan settled the expense. If Rebecca insisted that Eddie had a wife, the appropriate action would have been to hand his money over to her.

With the incredible aura surrounding this documentary, neither of the parties involved offered any assistance towards his burial. Two years after his passing, he remained in a box in Jessica's office closet. The interest in Eddie as a human being had been lost. His prearranged funeral plans of being buried next to his previous wife were well known but totally discarded. To this day, I still do not know where Eddie's remains are.

Unfortunately, Eddie's nephew also passed away before I could publish this book. Thankfully, he left us with some valuable information to paint a clearer picture.

Hidden Layers

- Mom's house was vacant for three years prior to the events shown in the documentary.
- Two of my siblings never lived in that house growing up. I was the youngest in high school and spent four years there. Rebecca lived there for a short time before leaving to go to college.
- The filming took place in several different physical locations provided by Rebecca. All scattered throughout Virginia and DC. The film may lead you to believe they were in Mom's house the entire time.
- Rebecca could have cared for the elders in her personal home in Virginia.
- The elders being in the home even for film purposes was against court orders.
- Mom weighed 112 pounds when she left with Rebecca in April 2014. Mom weighed 98 pounds upon her return to Florida in December 2014.
- On multiple occasions speaking with Mom via telephone, she would communicate that she was hungry.
- Mom was very tired of running up and down the road, and became malnourished. Rebecca discontinued administering Mom's prescribed medications without the consent of her doctors.
- Eddie lived in his nephew's townhome in Virginia.
- Eddie was welcomed and extended many invitations to accompany Mom on the scheduled visit to Florida witnessed in the documentary.
- Co-guardian/conservators hold a responsibility to inform each other of major changes such as a new marital status.

- Family members from multiple parties were upset with the documentary. Eddie's niece and nephew were upset with Rebecca.
- Cher's legal counsel assisted Rebecca in the beginning. In the end, Rebecca represented herself.
- A minimum wage case best describes the income allotted to Jessica for her responsibilities. She never tried to "steal" anything from my family or mother.
- It is not revealed the true difficulties presented to Jessica as she attempted to communicate and work with Rebecca.
- In the documentary, Rebecca asked Jessica if she ever met Mom. The facts are: no, Jessica never met her. But that was due to Rebecca actively avoiding and eluding Jessica, never making Mom available.

The creators of the documentary got a huge win that I will acknowledge later. Virginia only recognizes one invasion of privacy law. The law is the reason the Edith+Eddie documentary lives on today even though it is nonfactual. From my interpretation of privacy rights, I believe the filming of a private family matter is a total invasion. The filming turned into this huge fiasco. Virginia and New York have similar invasion of privacy laws, and Laura Checkoway was based in New York. When it comes to Mom, the court system appeared to be broken to the public, but in private the system was in fact correct on how they protected her. On the other hand, when I attempted to sue, the outcome created another victim. A real Hollywood tale.

10

Edith + Eddie

(The Documentary)

The documentary that has garnered millions of views on YouTube and Facebook is simply not accurate. It was published on YouTube by Topic on February 8th, 2018, and on Facebook by Real Stories on June 19th, 2021. Viewing estimates range upward of 20 million views so far across all platforms.

Wow!

Mom made it to the Academy Awards. Imagine having to sit in front of your TV and make the decision. Do you want your mom to win and make history even though it is a false story? Or would you want the documentary to lose because you were painted as the villain when you were the protector? I made a call to the Academy the night before to give my truth. Surprised to speak to a live person, I questioned the responsibility of the Academy in reference to validity of true facts contained in the documentary. They said that was all on the director. Ultimately, the documentary lost to another short film.

I break down the original film from 0:00 to 29:41 in its entirety. What is seen vs reality, facts vs fiction. Time slots may vary based on the version viewed. Hopefully the insight gives the viewers a new level of understanding of the editing used to create the film. Had I known a film was being created with this narrative, I would have done more visual documentation to prove my side of this situation. In the moment, I was only trying to take care of our mother, not prove any points. I only have my word, court records, and countless loved ones willing to tell the truth.

0:00 – 1:00

The documentary opens up with Mom and Eddie dancing in a bar. Two elders in their mid-90s out at a lounge in the blistering cold weather of Virginia, may not necessarily be a good idea. Yes, you want them to be happy and live out life on their terms. But that is not what is happening here. For the purposes of film, they are dragged out and asked to dance. That could be done in the warmth of a cozy home. Family members were constantly reaching out to spend time with Mom. Uncle Hubbard went to one of the bars where they were filming in order to spend time with Mom as that was the only way to meet up with her at that time. He describes the scene as loud and obnoxious, sitting directly next to a speaker, making it almost impossible to have any conversation with her. He said it was so loud the table was shaking. The family as a whole expected Mom to be in a more appropriate environment.

1:00 – 2:00

The story is told about how they actually met. Lewis was taking care of Mom when Eddie officially met them, and he told another story. Similar, but contrary to the one mentioned in the film. In the documentary Eddie says that he played a number Mom recommended to him, and they split $5,000. That is simply not true, that amount was incorporated for dramatics. It is unknown how much Eddie actually won. But it was verified by Lewis and Uncle Hubbard that Eddie gave Lewis and Mom $250 apiece. The number came out years after they met. It was not the fairy tale meet and greet, play the lotto, win and split story mentioned in the news and in the documentary.

Eddie did give Mom a few blouses from his previous wife as he mentioned. The "love at first sight" is questionable. Mom never once mentioned to me that she was in love with Eddie. She always referred to him as her new friend, before and after she was declared mentally incapacitated. Eddie mentioned to me personally that he would never marry again as it would ruin his retirement. Because I am neither of the two individuals, I can only go off of what each of them have consistently communicated to me. Facts are, in the scene, Eddie is doing all of the talking.

That is because Mom is no longer able to hold a full conversation and consistent thought. The filmmakers and my sister Rebecca understand this, that is why Mom does not do any of the story telling in the entire film.

Eddie seems to be reading from a script for the purpose of the film. After Eddie's claim of love at first sight, they use a film technique and voice-over to make it appear that Mom responds immediately. Her lips did not move in that scene. His lips were not saying the words you hear. It is clear she said "it was" at another moment in time and they aligned her voice in a response. Personally, I believe the tone of her voice is a giveaway to the notion of deception. The answer had none of the enthusiasm you would expect from someone "in love."

2:00 – 3:00

This scene opens up in Rebecca's beach house. To put it in perspective, this house is more than two hours away from Mom's home. Which means she is far away from any other local relative. Eddie walks into the kitchen with her dentures, which soak in a solution overnight, and has Mom place them in her mouth. It is not known if the dentures were properly rinsed off before she inserted them, but in the documentary you can clearly see her frown. This leads me to believe the solution was still on her teeth. I was bothered by the communication between Mom and Eddie, the tapping and shoving gesture of the casing towards her was unnecessary.

When she was under my care, I washed them off at the sink, gently placed them in her hand and helped her place them in her mouth. Letting her know that we were about to eat breakfast was more than enough motivation for her.

3:00 – 4:00

This scene briefly opens up at a church. It is unclear where the service was located. The exercise scene was in Rebecca's house in Northern Virginia. I had no issue with them exercising if it's under the appropriate supervision. I am under the belief that there was no professional guidance. As Mom jokingly said her ankles can break. I used a professional service that employed stabilizing equipment to safely secure Mom while they exercised her twice a week.

4:00 – 5:00

The news station is reporting the false story that Rebecca is spewing. They are also reporting the false narrative of the winning lotto ticket. In the documentary, it shows the news report where Rebecca said I was fighting for money and the house. I was fighting for what was right. Rebecca made many strategic moves over the years which indicated her desires to gain Mom's house and money along with Eddie's.

Mom is quoted saying *"she's not going to separate us, this man and me."* One thing I will mention is that she did not actually say Eddie's name. And a scene like this one was only displayed once even though they were filmed for multiple months on end. Therefore, it is unclear whether Mom knows that she is sitting next to Eddie or her second husband as he had a similar appearance to Eddie. Anyone dealing with dementia patients understands how they revert back to their past life. If Mom ever gave any indication of being in love with Eddie, I would not have a problem with it. The problem is being blindsided by a situation that never was.

The news reporter says that I was fighting Rebecca for full custody. How would they be privy to that information without Rebecca telling them? We recently became co-guardians, I was under the assumption that we were working together, but Rebecca was actually setting up an imaginary scenario. While I was in Florida awaiting my mother's return for an important medical appointment, my sister was betraying me to anyone who would listen.

Rebecca also makes the ridiculous claim that race played a role in my actions. For the record, I am not racist and never have been. I have a biracial grandson. Eddie could have been purple for all I cared. My actions would have been the same. Protect my mother. Selling her house was not a thought on my mind.

5:00 – 7:00

This scene opens up at Mom's residence. Rebecca is reading the mail sent to the address. She openly admits that she is no longer Mom's guardian. But she does not explain why she is no longer the guardian. Her actions caused the courts to remove her. At this point the house was vacant. There was no reason for anyone to be there other than the guardian and anyone assigned the task of renovating the property. Rebecca introduces the world to Jessica Neisen. Rebecca also downplays the condition of her mother saying she had mild dementia when it was more severe.

Rebecca also admits that she was power of attorney at one point but, like before, does not explain why she was removed. APS revoked her power of attorney. She goes on to say that none of her sisters had a close relationship with Mom. Rebecca had the benefit of general vicinity. She was closer in location, not in relationship. The marriage of the elders had no bearing on whether any of us received our inheritance; Eddie had no family who could threaten that situation.

At approximately 6:32, they show a pile of photos consisting of various things. At 6:34, they show Mom's second husband, Mr. Hill. Rebecca makes mention of where Mom wants to close her eyes. There have been many occasions in which my mother could not recall her own residence. Even in the documentary you can see how spaced out she appears at the end of this scene. Neither Rebecca nor I could decide where she ultimately ended up, since neither of us had the authority anymore.

7:00 – 9:00

This scene opens up with Rebecca stating that Mom was in love at first sight. Again, furthering the narrative of a love story. She was not there when Mom and Eddie met to make such claims. Only my brother Lewis had the perspective of witnessing this event. Neither he nor Mom ever stated that it was love at first sight. Eddie, for that matter, never said anything like that until cameras were in his face for a documentary. I am not here to say who was in love or not, but I will give the insight that was given to me.

During an interview with Laura Checkoway that was conducted by Stephen Saito, he asked, *"There's a beautiful moment where the two sit by the water and talk. You clearly knew it would be significant since it's shot from a number of different angles, but where did that instinct come from?"*

Checkoway's response was, *"Seeing them together, being lucky enough to witness their love, you knew you were in the presence of something special, so listening to that conversation felt poignant and powerful. I love that scene because it shows both of their personalities."*

Saito then asks, *"In general is getting that across something difficult to achieve in the edit?"*

Checkoway's response was, *"Edith has mild dementia and Eddie is hard of hearing, so I think that shaped some of what we got. The story almost dictated the edit itself in a certain way. Of course, there's a lot of crafting that we do, but I just try to stay as close to the truth as possible. We were in this bubble of love with Edith and Eddie and then that bubble is burst and things unfolded as they did."*

The scene these questions refer to takes place at Rebecca's beach house. Mom and Eddie are on the cold river bank alone. This scene bothered me due to the safety of the elders. One of them could have easily gotten up from their chairs, wandered off, and slid down the shoreline. Within the same scene, there is a canopy tent at 8:20 that is not properly extended or planted within the ground. The elders are literally one gust of wind away from injury. This shows the constant negligence of Rebecca and the film crew. The actions are best for making a "movie," not what was in the elder's best interest—and certainly not what was natural between the two. Eddie is even heard saying, "worry about falling in the water."

The conversation really highlights the nature of my mother's dementia. Checkoway says that my mother's dementia was mild. Mom was already three years into a moderate diagnosis which means she was further along in the seven stages of the disease. That is distinctly different from saying mild dementia which downplays the severity. Mom hadn't lived alone without assistance for several years to that point. She was not responding directly to Eddie. And he was not necessarily doing so either. Mom said, "If you see somebody that need help, help them." And that I did. At the time, I was unaware those words were being said, but help was on the way.

9:00 – 11:30

This scene opens up at the Community United Methodist Church in D.C. Mom rarely attended any church in that area. Minister Drummond is not our cousin or bloodline as stated in the documentary. This adds to the illusion that family was involved. She is speaking on family affairs that she is unaware of, and has no insight into the severity of the situation. She thanks Rebecca, her children, and grandchildren as if they were heroes. Rebecca did not have any grandchildren at the time of filming. Rebecca, Robin, and Edna played a role in the manipulation of the story. They are the only members of our family with a voice in the film. Unfortunately, for all the people who watched the documentary, the directors allowed them to spew this flawed storyline.

I want to highlight that Mom had one living brother, two other living daughters, eight grown grandchildren, and ten great grandchildren ranging from children to grown adults. None of whom were in attendance or invited. None of whom were aware of a "marriage." The directors took this opportunity to "plug" their company into the film. There is a voiceover of Eddie saying, "The heart is red," which is "coincidently" the same name as Checkoway's nonprofit company. Mom's sister Edna was also in this scene, she had memory issues and was gullible. Through research and retracing family history, I have come to the realization that Edna would go along with any of Rebecca's actions in the past. And it appeared she went down that same road for this documentary. Eddie ends the scene with the compelling statement, **"We went to Reverend Cole, where we been going to church, and he married us. And they're trying to say it's not legal. They think they're gonna wear us down but they're not gonna wear us down. We married for life."** Eddie's statement is misguided and not true.

11:30 – 12:30

This scene opens up with Rebecca and Robin on the porch of Mom's house. She says, *"I was called by my lawyer and told that my sister may come and pick them up."* By stating this, she is clearly acknowledging that I am in town to pick up our mother, an event which had been previously arranged through her guardian. At this time, a love scene was the last thing on my mind. Again, because our mother never acknowledged Eddie as more than a "friend," I was more concerned with the safety and wellbeing of Mom. Eddie was invited, but he chose to stay in Virginia. Rebecca goes on to tell lie after lie in this part of the film. The ugliest accusation she comes up with is calling my husband abusive. She states that I am looking to sell the house when I have absolutely no power to do so. Her daughter Robin ends the scene making the statement, *"I decided you just put it in God's hands."* She is "acting" as if she is crying but no tears are there. Robin knows that she never called her grandmother one time after the making of this documentary.

12:30 – 14:00

This scene opens up with Mom seemingly saying goodbye to everyone. They all prayed in the living room of Mom's home. She knew Reverend Cole in the film because my brother Lewis would take her to his church occasionally. She also knew a different Reverend Cole from Christiansburg in her early days. Mom would often reference the Reverend Cole from her early adult life. Although not shown in the film, I wanted family members to be present before Mom went to Florida. This scene should have been actual family members instead of Rebecca's acquaintances. It is confirmed by Uncle Hubbard that Rebecca told him not to come earlier that day.

Mom says, *"Where's Eddie?"* It appears that everyone in the room is grasping for a moment that just did not happen. The woman says, *"She's worried about him."* Well, if this is a documentary about a married couple, why is this surprising? And why are they trying to emphasize this moment? They were friends, and my mother is a loving person by nature, it is no surprise that she displayed hospitality by wanting to pray with Eddie. This is good-bye scene number one.

14:00 – 15:30

The drama unfolds when the fully clothed elders were placed in bed side by side anticipating and preparing for the "evil" people coming to separate them. Neither elder was capable of understanding the real dangers they were facing in their current environment. Rebecca coerced and manipulated the elders with a promise to take care of both.

After I witnessed the documentary with the world, I wondered why they moved them upstairs to the bed. Notice the elders had the same clothes on from the scene before. Rebecca mentioned in the scene earlier that she was aware I was on the way to pick Mom up. We all were supposed to meet at the steak house in town. When that did not happen, we responded accordingly. Upon watching the film over and over, trying to make sense of everything, I am under the impression they moved the elders upstairs for the sole purpose of dramatics. More tactics and antics by Rebecca and the film crew to get a reaction out of everyone. The house was deemed unsafe by court orders. No one should have been in the house, especially the elders.

Rebecca placed the phone in Mom's hand while Jessica was on the line. Mom asks if they ever met, but contact was limited or nonexistent due to Rebecca. I know my mother well, when the phone magically appeared in Eddie's hand, I knew she had no idea who he was in that moment. I can see the look on her face. Multiple times throughout the documentary I can see her look of confusion.

One intense moment came about when Rebecca continued to push the ugly lie of abuse. Since I knew the truth, it was clear that Rebecca instilled lies into our mother's head. It was astonishing to hear Mom repeat what had been drilled into her and practiced for film purposes.

Rebecca: *"Did Rayfield push you while you were there?"*

Mom: *"Yeah, he pushed me, tried to make me clean."*

Rebecca: *"Did he put his hands on you and push you?"*

Mom: *"Put my hand, yeah. Hands on the rag or something. He decided he want to make me do some work."*

I responded to her claim with "OK, now did he pay you?"

The officers present chuckled at her response. I was edited out of that conversation in the documentary. My assessment is that Rebecca used a borderline intimidation tactic on our mother during that conversation by interjecting, instead of allowing her to naturally speak. Rebecca had to make sure Mom said the right things. This was the turning point for me. The gloves are completely off. In that powerful moment, I knew this was heading in the wrong direction. It was one thing to hear the lie from your sister's mouth. It is a completely different feeling to witness it come from your mother's mouth, knowing she was manipulated.

15:30 – 17:00

The scene continues with Rebecca now downstairs in the kitchen maintaining the dramatics. I could not help but notice she had a different phone in her hand other than the one they were just using. The phone being passed around had an orange casing; she is now using a black phone with the lawyer. The lawyer is telling her who has the authority in the situation. Remember, Rebecca had power over Mom that was revoked multiple times. She repeatedly resorts to the abuse claims to hopefully regain control.

Rebecca seemed to cast a spell on our aunt Edna, Mom's sister. They both were cut from the same cloth. Edna is in the window looking out and talking about the situation. Edna mentions that Mom does not need to be going up and down the road, but it was Rebecca who took them back and forth throughout Virginia. Mom's brother supported the move to Florida. And now for obvious reasons, Uncle Hubbard was told not to show as he would have interfered with the filming of the documentary, where as Edna went right along.

17:00 – 21:00

The documentary continues showing a clear shot of me and Jessica. I turned my back on the film crew as they were pointing cameras in my direction. I feel the directors are now truly invading our privacy as they show our faces and place our names side by side. Neither one of us gave consent to be in the film. When I realized Rebecca was resisting, I called the police to the scene. That is the reason they appear in the documentary. It was a good thing I did. I may not have been able to rescue my mother if it had not been for them. Jessica arrived with the proper paperwork to validate and show that what was happening was official.

The officers asked if there were any firearms in the house because Mom's home was filled with acquaintances of Rebecca. My brother Lewis, at one point, had legal firearms that were missing. So to that question, I answered "I don't know." She had a strategic group of people in the home as if this was a final good-bye. The presence of some of the members made little to no sense, unless of course your true goal is to create a tear-jerking documentary.

Police entered, cleared out the house and questioned folks. Eddie is heard saying that they do not want to go to Florida because "Pam" is trying to sell the house. Eddie was speaking on things that he would have no clue about unless Rebecca told him to say it. Jessica then reiterates the urgency of time. To the public it may sound like she was being rude, but she was being straightforward knowing the last flights of the night were approaching. Understanding her ward was in a bad situation, Jessica had to be firm to get her point across. Eddie then says that our mother lived in the house her entire life, and raised her children there, which is simply not accurate. The lies are not matching up and do not make sense when you know the truth. And Rebecca is the puppet master.

The powerful sequences end with Eddie telling Jessica, **"You'll remember this to your dying day. You will remember this until your dying day."** In fact he may be correct. If we are blessed enough to retain our memories until our time comes, this will be something we will remember forever. Not because we did anything wrong, but for the reason of successfully saving our mother.

21:00 – 23:30

We are forced to walk Mom out in the rain, since everything took longer than expected due to the chaos. We entered our rental car and drove off into the proverbial sunset—or rather, a literal rain storm. We are never recorded or filmed by them again. Mom known to be mild and sweet, but feisty if you get on her bad side, had no opposition to leaving with me to go to Florida.

At that time, I had no idea what their true motive was in filming a scheduled transfer. And never once thought I'd be writing a book about it. But whoa! Was I in for a surprise. Jessica, my husband, and I appear to be villains.

Eddie is seen being filmed in Mom's house against court orders. The film blatantly lies by stating that Eddie is unable to reach Mom. The phone lines were always open, and they did have conversations.

23:30 – 27:30

This scene opens up with Eddie shown on life support after he collapsed. Eddie had known health issues. The IV bag shown in the documentary displays 5% dextrose. This is used to treat low blood sugar and dehydration. Which treats some of his exact ailments. Under Rebecca's care, he was also malnourished. Doctors explained that his blood counts were off which indicated that he may not have been taking his medicine properly. I have factual evidence that our mother was taken off her medicine which leads me to believe that Eddie was taken off his as well.

Out of respect for Eddie, I will not reveal the true cause of death. Although I cannot say whether he truly had a broken heart, I will say that his death certificate states otherwise.

While in the hospital, it was later discovered that someone cleared Eddie's bank account. The only names on his account were his and Rebecca. I truly believe had it not been for Rebecca and the film crew running the two elders up and down the road in freezing rainy conditions, Eddie may have lived much longer. There was never a point within the couple of weeks Mom was in Florida that Eddie could not talk to her. There was also no mention that she would never return. That is, unless Rebecca was feeding him lies.

If you need a snapshot of the crazy I had to deal with, take this quote verbatim from Rebecca in the last scenes: ***"With the dementia, sure she forgets but sometimes it's important to forget as it is to remember, and as long as she remembers who he is and that he was her husband or is her husband, then she should be afforded the opportunity to say good-bye."***

All jokes aside, Mom did not remember she was married as soon as we arrived at the airport—and she may have never truly known she was married. Even in the film, she never once says that she is married.

Part of this scene is a powerful prayer by Reverend Cole. Through an interview conducted by Stephen Saito the question is asked, *"There was a mesmerizing shot of the Reverend Cole's leading a prayer near the end – what kind of lens did you use for that?"*

Checkoway's response was, *"That scene was shot on the 5D, which the rest of the film was not because we had to sneak into [that location] and the 5D is small. So the way that it looks is just by chance, but it really works."*

Again, Eddie the human being is lost here. Why did the director feel the need to film a man in a vulnerable moment. To go as far as sneaking a camera in the hospital in order to film this scene lacks a moral compass. Put the camera down if you really care about him. At some point, morals, integrity, and sound principals should take precedence over simply "getting the shot."

27:30 – 29:41

The documentary ends with Mom singing a song popular within the family. It is well known that her very first boyfriend sang that song to her. They would literally go out under an evergreen tree on the banks of a river in Riner, Virginia. She can recall that song instantly.

✳ ✳ ✳

While the documentary was released and moving across the world, I was still cleaning up the mess behind the scenes. I want to take a moment to discuss a popular topic brought up in the documentary. The results of what happened to Mom's home. Rebecca said I was trying to take the home for myself. By now I believe I have proven, at the very least, that the home was not my top priority. Unless Cher was going to keep her promise to renovate the home. Making sure our mother spent her final years in a suitable environment was my main focus.

So for anyone wondering, after Mom's passing, I entered probate and liquidated the home. Due to a large lien against my mother's property, I was forced to sell her house. I only had six months to do so as the creditors would be looking for payment plus interest. Every time we went to court for a dispute, those charges were added to the estate. The remaining profits of the estate were divided up amongst all the siblings and other family members. Yes, even after all this, Rebecca got her fair share of the estate. This is how any inheritances across the world should function within a family unless there is a trust or will in place.

This is exactly what Mom wanted, minus the drama.

11

The Circulatory System

*A*lexandria Circuit Court. Case number CL1800-1993

Virginia Statute (Code Section 8.01.40):

Unauthorized use of name or picture of any person; punitive damages; statute of limitations.

A. Any person whose name, portrait, or picture is used without having first obtained the written consent of such person, or if dead, of the surviving consort and if none, of the next of kin, or if a minor, the written consent of his or her parent or guardian, for advertising purposes or for the purposes of trade, such persons may maintain a suit in equity against the person, firm, or corporation so using such person's name, portrait, or picture to prevent and restrain the use thereof; and may also sue and recover damages for any injuries sustained by reason of such use. And if the defendant shall have knowingly used such person's name, portrait or picture in such manner as is forbidden or declared to be unlawful by this chapter, the jury, in its discretion, may award punitive damages.

B. No action shall be commenced under this section more than 20 years after the death of such person.

After viewing the documentary, a decision was made to contact an attorney. I interviewed three separate attorneys. Each of which advised that a defamation and/or slander case would be hard to prevail. One attorney suggested that we might seek a case based on privacy and publicity rights. He pulled court records, realized how complex the circumstances were, and decided to take the case.

With evidence stacked to the ceiling, the lawyer moved forward with legal action against Cher, Rebecca, Laura Checkoway, Kartemquin, and others all for their roles in the production of Edith + Eddie. Their roles collectively assisted with the popularity of the film. Cher, the fairy godmother, eventually signed on as an executive producer. Laura Checkoway is the director, and Kartemquin films is the producer. And, of course, Rebecca is the mastermind of it all. Clearly I was the underdog facing the high-powered lawyers of celebrities and directors. All parties were subpoenaed and required to present their case. What I believed to be irrefutable proof of wrongdoing, in the court of law, just was not enough.

According to the defense lawyer's interpretation of the law, it does not matter if the story displayed me in a false light. That is not enough to bring forth a complaint of invasion of privacy in the state of Virginia. Claims as such are extremely limited in common law or otherwise. Their lawyers repeatedly stated in court that what was portrayed in the film was truthful. If I were to put a number on it, 90% of the details presented in the film were misleading to some degree. The lawyers made references to documentary films such as Super Size Me and Anyplace But Here, where Candelria and Delan both brought lawsuits against the respective filmmakers, but to no avail.

All of a sudden, the narrative has shifted from romance to elder abuse within the guardianship system. The reason it changed was that they wanted a backhanded way to sell the story, both literally and figuratively. By claiming elder abuse, it added another element to enhance the newsworthy aspect of the story. Their lawyers stated the right of individual privacy comes secondhand to the public's right to have free distribution of news and information. Due to this new storyline, Jessica also took a fall. Simply doing her job landed her on a scorching hot seat in the eyes of the public. Jessica is a hero who helped me save my mother, as far as I am concerned.

The court's decision was that the documentary has "newsworthy" components, and the public has a "right to know." A demurrer was sustained, as the courts decided there was not enough merit to support the case.[23] It was the main defense of Virginia's privacy law. A decision that ultimately is the reason you are reading this book today. After the court system handed down this judgement, I felt compelled to reveal the truth.

The opposing lawyers admit that the film starts a conversation, but the conversation is misconstrued. It should not be solely about elder abuse, interracial marriage, or intra-family issues, as they claim. The conversation should also be about how the Virginia court system allowed them, as filmmakers, to intrude on private family matters, produce a documentary without all parties' permission, and profit from it without consequences, all while presenting a nonfactual film. They even state in their court papers that just because a film is created with the intention of increasing sales, it does not determine whether the production is used for advertising or trade purposes. They claim that having intentions for profit does not negate one's right to depict a matter of public interest.

I believe that, at the outset, some parties were innocently manipulated. As time went on, I found it hard to believe they were unaware that something was amiss, which reinforced my decision to fight for what was ethical. The determination extends beyond me. I fought for my family who needed to see it through. Also, for elders all around the world.

This is a way directors, and all parties involved can invade a family's privacy, but also reap the profits from the story as well without paying Mom or Eddie or their estates. Everyone has either made money or advanced their careers on the back of this false story. Even after filing a lawsuit, these individuals did not relent. As previously stated, they continued to release the short documentary on additional social media platforms, further advancing the story and spreading a false narrative. To this day, I have not heard a single word from them attempting to rectify this situation.

For The Love of Money

I have my own questions I'd like to share.

- Why wait until Mom passed to market the documentary?
- Who exactly profited from the film?
- Why was Eddie filmed in the hospital at such a vulnerable moment?
- Why were the film makers not interested in the other side of the story?
- Who received the "gifts" from all the awards the documentary was winning?

I believe these are valid questions, and hopefully, anyone interested in this story shares the same sentiments. My efforts to convey the truth were unsuccessful. I cannot reach any of them, so perhaps the power of the public can!

Neither Mom nor Eddie received any compensation for their "actor" roles in the documentary. They promoted the newsworthy aspect but also made it available for sale through various media platforms and other channels. I believe the only people who benefited were pursuing their own agendas.

12
Family Anatomy

July 16th, 1918: Edith is born in Riner, VA.

1938: Edith marries first husband, Lewis McDaniel.

January 29th, 1939: Edith's first child, Lewis, is born.

August 7th, 1940: Ernestine (Tina) is born.

March 21st, 1944: Rebecca is born.

February 10th, 1947: Patricia is born.

1951: Edith divorces first husband, Mr. McDaniel.

Mid-1950s: Edith marries second husband, our stepfather, William Hill.

1960: Edith and William Hill purchase house seen in documentary.

1961/62: Mr. Hill passes away.

1965 — 1985: Edith and companion, Henry, lived in house seen in documentary.

2004: Edith's cousin, Mitchell, moves in to provide additional security.

2007: Lewis moves in house to take care of her. Edith and Lewis meet Eddie Harrison.

April 30th, 2010: Rebecca revises Edith's will.

September 2010: Lewis asked me for help to review Edith's bank accounts because money was missing.

November 1st, 2010: Edith unknowingly signs power of attorney over to Rebecca.

January 3, 2011: Edith's Mini Mental Exam is performed by her physician and reveals significant loss of function in multiple domains of cognition.

June 2011: Email sent to protective services concerning the money Rebecca removed from Mom's account.

July 2011: Rebecca's power of attorney is revoked.

August 2011: Edith officially declared mentally incapacitated with dementia by a court.

November 2011 — Feb 2014: Edith lived with Tina in Maryland, leaving her home in Virginia vacant.

May 2012 – Dec 2012: Edith visits me in Florida and is diagnosed with breast cancer by a Florida doctor.

January 2013: Tina's lawyer advised her that Edith had to return to her care and responsibility.

February 2014: Courts award co-guardian status to Rebecca and me.

March 2014 – April 2014: Courts place Edith in Florida with me until renovations are complete.

April 2014 – December 6th, 2014: Rebecca takes Edith back to Virgina. Edith and Eddie are married under her care. The documentary is created.

August 2014: Court assigns third party, Jessica Niesen, as guardian.

December 6th, 2014 – March 21st, 2017: Edith's scheduled visit to Florida was granted by Jessica. Edith returns to Florida with me.

December 30th, 2014: Eddie passes away.

March 21st, 2017: Edith passes away.

13

Heart of War

(Art of War)

Mom, Eddie, Jessica, my husband, and I were all taken advantage of in some form or fashion for the development of this film. In a sense, even the public could be considered victims of manipulation. The twenty-nine-minute documentary fabricated a story that won film festivals and nominations for both Oscar and Emmy awards. However, the short film is not the true story of Edith and Eddie. The court of public opinion can hit you like a ton of bricks, especially when they accuse you of wrongdoing. Film makers and producers release a film to the world which introduces elements of black vs white, care vs abuse, honesty vs deception, and power vs the helpless all to create an ugly narrative. With that, I felt obligated to rebuke the images portrayed in the documentary even if it's an ugly truth.

Simply put, marriage after cognitive decline is not ideal. Under law, a person declared mentally incapacitated is not supposed to be able to make life-altering decisions on their own. Mom was in no state of mind to make a sound judgment to the extent of a marriage. She never lived with Eddie and could not remember who he was at times. The only time Eddie was an occupant of Mom's house was when there was a camera shoved in his face. Eddie never mentioned he was in love with Mom until he was being filmed, which was when he became the most vulnerable and Rebecca was there to take advantage. Eddie had little to no family and needed support and care. He was willing to do as told in order to be taken care of. That decision may well have cost him his life. A truly sad story.

The details embedded within this saga are mind blowing. All the twists and turns, ups and downs, mimic that of a fairytale but this is a piece of my life story. I could not possibly squeeze all aspects into this book. My sister found a way to create a real-life Hollywood movie through the betrayal of her own mother and family. Manipulating others and leading them with her "evil genius" ways. To our surprise and research, this was not her first time doing something like this. And from her history, I doubt it will be her last.

I, Patricia Barber, have nothing to hide.

This is the good, bad, and ugly truth!

P.S.: If anyone suddenly enters a loved one's life at an old age, watch out! Especially if it's my sister Rebecca.

In loving memory of Edith, Eddie, and family.

Sources

Dunks, Glenn. "Every Movie Nominated for an Oscar This Year, Ranked from Worst to Best." Junkee, 4 Mar. 2018, archive.junkee.com/every-oscar-nominee-ranked/148691. #49 Edith+Eddie Nominated for: Documentary Short

Edith+Eddie. Directed by Laura Checkoway. Produced by Thomas Lee Wright. Executive producer Cher. USA: Kartemquin Films, 2017. Film.

Gardner, Chris. "Cher Backs Interracial Couple's Doc Award Season Hopes." The Hollywood Reporter, The Hollywood Reporter, 21 Sept. 2017, www.hollywoodreporter.com/movies/movie-news/cher-backs-interracial-couples-doc-awards-season-1041092/.

Saito, Stephen. "'Edith+Eddie' Director Laura Checkoway on Filming with Compassion." The Moveable Fest, 10 Mar. 2017, moveablefest.com/laura-checkoway-edith-and-eddie/.

of Justice, US Department. "Elder Abuse and Elder Financial Exploitation Statutes." Elder Justice Initiative (EJI) | Elder Abuse and Elder Financial Exploitation Statutes | United States Department of Justice, 17 Oct. 2023, www.justice.gov/elderjustice/prosecutors/statutes.

of Justice, US Department. "Red Flags of Elder Abuse." Elder Justice Initiative (EJI), 7 Nov. 2023, www.justice.gov/elderjustice/red-flags-elder-abuse.

*Superscripted numbers correspond to the matching document number. 1-23

Some documents support the story although not directly referenced.

Appendix

Contains documents mentioned in this book. documents are listed in chronological order. Some may not be directly referenced. Sensitive information redacted.

Document 1
Recommendation for Power of Attorney
(Letter confirming moderate dementia)

Bibhuti B. Mishra, MD, MRCP (UK)

Neurology • EMG • EEG • Evoked Potentials

Whittier Avenue ■ McLean, VA 22101 ■ TEL 703.356.   . ■ Fax 703.356

January 3, 2011

Re: Edith Hill
DOB: 07/16/1918

To Whom It May Concern:

Ms. Hill was sent by her physician Ambrish Gupta for evaluation of memory loss. Examination including Mini Mental Status Examination reveals she has significant loss of function in multiple domains of cognition. Her Mini Mental Status Examination Score is 12/30 which is consistent with moderate degree form of dementia. In addition to that, her MRI of the brain revealed moderate cortical atrophy and small vessel disease consistent with either Alzeihmer's disease or arteriosclerotic dementia. She is currently taking Aricept and Namenda for her dementia, and is being referred to home health care for medication management, assistance with activities of daily living, blood pressure monitoring, physical therapy and gait training.

I recommend a power of attorney to be responsible for her personal and financial affairs because of her difficulty managing personal affairs, forgetfulness, difficulty remembering and difficulty looking after herself.

Please call at (703) 356-   for questions or concerns. Thank you.

Sincerely,

Bibhuti B. Mishra, MD, MRCP
Mellanie P. Medina, FNP-BC

Document 2
E-mail request to Adult Protective Services
(Expressing concerns over Mom's well-being)

Problematic... (possibly unneccessary) stress continuing on elderly person (Edith Hill)

Patricia Barber   6/20/11
To veldaweathers@ .gov

From: **pebarber@ .com**
Saved: Mon 6/20/11 9:27 PM
To: veldaweathers@ .gov

June 20, 2011

Dear Ms. Weathers,

Is there something in place the retrieve my mothers money?? This matter is stressing her daily. I know you are not responsible for her emotions but, if
brother (Lewis) and you have a process that you are working on PLEASE LET ME KNOW. He does not seem to be fully aware of the process OR he cannot explain it .....only that he is waiting for you.

If a better plan (or different plan) would speed up this process , please let me know that also. Is there another avenue for me to take???

I am in the process of making travel arrangements for the 2nd week of July, 2011.. If possible, I would like to meet with you ...or.. someone in your absence. This is not a matter of sibling rivalry from my standpoint, but in order for you to make concrete valid decisions concerning my mother's welfare some information is needed that you are not aware of ...I am concerned about the well being of my mother. I'm certainly not sure that you understood the depth of our last conversation which I thought was confidential.

I would appreciate it if you would call me concerning the daily stress being placed on my mother (Ms. Hill   Princess Street).

Document 3
Petition for appointment of Co-guardians and co-conservators

The series of complaints against Lewis from Rebecca prompted the city of Alexandria to move to appoint co-guardians/conservators.

VIRGINIA:

IN THE CIRCUIT COURT OF THE CITY OF ALEXANDRIA

CITY OF ALEXANDRIA,

        Petitioner

v.   Fiduciary No. CL11001379

EDITH HILL,

        Respondent

PETITION FOR APPOINTMENT OF
CO-GUARDIANS AND CO-CONSERVATORS

    COMES NOW Petitioner City of Alexandria, by counsel, pursuant to Section 37.2-1000 et *seq.* of the Code of Virginia, as amended, and moves this Honorable Court for entry of an Order appointing co-guardians and co-conservators for Edith Hill, and states as follows:

    1. Petitioner City of Alexandria is acting through its Adult Protective Services unit,

        Alexandria, Virginia 22301.

    2. Respondent Edith Hill is 92 years old, and her birth date is July 16, 1918.

    3. Ms. Hill resides at   Street,

Alexandria, Virginia   , which is her mailing address.

4. Ms. Hill is suffering from cognitive impairment and dementia, as noted in the attached report of Bibhuti B. Mishra, M.D., a physician who has evaluated Ms. Hill. Dr. Mishra in his report is of the opinion that Ms. Hill's condition prevents her from managing her own personal and financial affairs and attending to her own health needs. A copy of the report of Dr. Mishra concerning Ms. Hill is filed under seal with this Petition.

5. Ms. Hill is widowed and has four children: Lewis McDaniel, Ernestine Yates, Rebecca Wright, and Patricia Barber. Notice of this proceeding is being given to each of the children as well as to Ms. Hill's brother Curtis Hubbard.

6. The Petitioner is aware of no other person to whom Ms. Hill has provided her power of attorney.

7. The Petitioner believes that Ms. Hill's estate consists of her residence, located at   , Alexandria, Virginia   , which has an assessed value of $492,677. Ms. Hill receives retirement benefits

of $1343 monthly from Social Security and approximately $500 monthly from the Arlington County School Board. She has accounts with unknown balances at SunTrust Bank. There may be an additional account at SunTrust set up by her daughter Rebecca Wright with a $9000 balance in Ms. Hill's name at SunTrust, but the situation with this account is not clear.

Ms. Hill may also own an interest in property located at   Road, Riner, Virginia   , but the status of the title to this property is also not clear.

8. The Petitioner believes that the Respondent's attendance at the hearing on this Petition would be detrimental to the Respondent's health, care and safety.

9. The Respondent's native language is English and no alternative mode of communication is required.

10. The Petitioner believes that Kenneth Labowitz and Anne Heishman are each an appropriate person to serve as Co-Guardian and Co-Conservator for Ms. Hill. Mr. Labowitz and Ms. Heishman are attorneys in private practice before the Bar of this Court, with extensive experience as a fiduciary and specifically as guardian

and conservator. Their office address is Street, Suite , Alexandria, Virginia . Their mailing address is Post Office Box , Alexandria, Virginia .

11. The plan for Ms. Hill's care following the appointment of the proposed Co-Guardians and Co-Conservators is to attempt to permit her to remain in her own home with additional assistance to protect her and ensure her safety and care.

WHEREFORE, Petitioner City of Alexandria respectfully prays that an Order be entered appointing a guardian ad litem to represent the interests of Edith Hill in this proceeding; that the Court enter an Order appointing Kenneth Labowitz and Anne Heishman as Co-Guardians and Co-Conservators for Ms. Hill, pursuant to §§ 37.2-1009 and -1013, respectively, of the Code of Virginia, as amended; and for such other relief that the Court finds Petitioner entitled.

(signature)
Kenneth E. Labowitz
    Virginia Bar No. 18580
Anne M. Heishman
    Virginia Bar No. 65540
Dingman Labowitz P.C.
    Street, Suite
Post Office Box
Alexandria, Virginia
703/519-
703/519-   fax

Counsel for Petitioner

Document 4
Report of Guardian AD Litem Guardian AD Litem

Julie recommends that the court appoint a guardian and conservator for Ms. Hill. She did not recommend Rebecca to be appointed sole guardian/conservator.

VIRGINIA:

IN THE CIRCUIT COURT OF THE CITY OF ALEXANDRIA

REBECCA M. WRIGHT,

    Petitioner

v.   Fiduciary No. CW11001267

EDITH HILL,

    Respondent

REPORT OF GUARDIAN AD LITEM

COMES NOW Julie C. Parks, Guardian ad litem for Edith Hill, and for her Report to the Petition for Appointment of Guardian and Conservator pursuant to §37.2-1003, Code of Virginia, as amended, states the following:

1. **Jurisdiction:** This Court has proper jurisdiction over Edith Hill pursuant to §37.2-1001(A). Ms. Hill resides at   Alexandria, Virginia.

2. **Service of Process:** On July 6, 2011 I personally served Ms. Hill at her home with copies of the Petition for Appointment of Guardian and Conservator, Notice of Hearing, and Order of Appointment of Guardian Ad Litem, as required in §37.2-1004(B).

3. **Physician's Evaluation:** An evaluation report was not filed with the Petition in this case, but I was able to review the evaluation report filed in the City of Alexandria's Petition for Appointment of Co-Guardians and Co-Conservators for Ms. Hill, CW11001379. Dr. Mishra, MD stated that Ms. Hill suffers from dementia and Alzeihmer's disease and has significant loss of function in multiple domains of cognition.

4. **Visit with Edith Hill:** I visited with Edith Hill on July 6, 2011 at her home in Alexandria. Ms. Hill is doing remarkable well for her age and we had a lengthy

conversation. I explained to Ms. Hill my role as Guardian ad litem and of her rights to contest the petition, attend the hearing, request a jury trial, compel witnesses, present evidence, and retain counsel, pursuant to §37.2-1006 and -1007. She explained that she has lived in her current home for about 50 years and for the last 5 years her son, Lewis McDaniel, has lived with her in the home. Mr. McDaniel prepares meals, pays the bills, runs errands, and takes Ms. Hill to her doctor's appointments and social events in the community. Ms. Hill is happy with the current arrangement and would like to continue to reside in her home as long as possible. She also stated that Mr. McDaniel should be appointed her Guardian and Conservator as he is already performing those duties. Ms. Hill was able to carry on a coherent conversation, name all of her children, and read and understand the Petition and Notice. She was able to answer general questions regarding her finances, but was unable to provide specifics about her monthly income and the property that she owns. Ms. Hill was able to move around the house quite easily. Her home is clean and comfortable, although Mr. McDaniel stated it does need some repair work.

5. **Conversation with Rebecca Wright, Petitioner:** The Petitioner is one of Ms. Hill's children. She is concerned that her mother is not receiving the appropriate amount of care, is being taken advantage of financially, and being mistreated by Mr. McDaniel. If Ms. Wright is appointed Guardian and Conservator her plan is to move to Northern Virginia and visit her mom daily to ensure she is being properly cared for. Despite Mr. Wright's concerns about her mother's living situation, Ms. Wright plans for her mother to continue to reside in her house with Mr. McDaniel until her health requires a different arrangement.

6. **Conversations with Rebecca Wright's Siblings:** I spoke with all three of Ms. Wright's siblings: Lewis McDaniel, Patricia Barbour, and Ernestine Yates. All three stated that Lewis McDaniel should serve as the Guardian and Conservator and expressed concern about appointing Rebecca Wright for those roles. Ms. Barbour and Ms. Yates are pleased with the level of care their brother provides for their mother; Mr. McDaniel has a nurse come to the home several times a week to help care for Ms. Hill as well as an extended family member who visits the home every day. All of the siblings are uneasy with an incident where Ms. Wright removed about $11,000 of Ms. Hill's money, which has not yet been returned. Ms. Barbour and Mr. McDaniel also expressed an interest in being appointed Guardian and Conservator.

7. **Asset and Financial Information:** I was able to confirm the allegations set forth in the Petition regarding Ms. Hill's assets. Her home on   Street in Alexandria has an assessed value of $492,677. She receives $1340 per month in Social Security and $500 per month from a pension with the Arlington County School Board. She has an account with Suntrust Bank with an average balance of a few thousand dollars. Ms. Hill also has a partial interest in some property located on   Road in Montgomery County, Virginia, which has an assessed value of $115,400.

8. **Recommendation as to Guardianship and Conservatorship:** I recommend that the Court appoint a Guardian and Conservator for Ms. Hill. Ms. Hill is unable to meet her health and safety needs without the assistance of a guardian. Additionally, Ms. Hill is unable to manage her financial affairs without the aid of a conservator. I further recommend that the right to sell or encumber real property in which Ms. Hill has an interest be permitted under the conservatorship, with this authority limited by the

requirement that the conservator seek the approval of the Court for any proposed contract of sale after notice to other relatives.

9. **Recommendation as to Identity of Guardian and Conservator:** At this time, I do not recommend that Rebecca Wright be appointed sole Guardian and Conservator. Ms. Hill's interests would be better served by appointing one of her other children as Guardian and Conservator, perhaps more than one, if an appropriate family member is willing to assume those responsibilities. Alternatively, a third party should be appointed Guardian and Conservator.

10. **Recommendation as to Bonds:** If Ms. Wright is appointed Guardian and Conservator, I recommend that the Guardians' bond be set at $1,000.00 without surety and that the Conservators' bond be set at $175,000.00, with surety.

11. **Content of Pleadings; Independent Counsel:** I reviewed the Petition and documents filed by the Petitioner. My investigation revealed nothing inconsistent with the facts asserted in the Petition.

Respectfully submitted,

Julie Pa
Julie C. Parks. Guardian ad litem
Parks & Schaffer, PLLC
Virginia State Bar No. 75282
PO Box
Alexandria VA
703-229-

Certificate of Mailing

I certify that a copy of the foregoing Report was sent by electronic mail or United States Mail, first class postage paid, upon the following persons, on July 8, 2011:

James DeVita
   Boulevard, Suite
Arlington, Virginia

Jeffrey Vogelman
   Street
Alexandria, Virginia

Rebecca Wright

Edith Hill

Lewis McDaniel

Ernestine Yates

Patricia Cullens Barbour

Kenneth Labowitz
Anne Heishman
   Street, Suite
Alexandria, Virginia

Julie C. Parks, Guardian ad litem

Document 5
Response and Opposition to petition for appointment of guardian and conservator

In this court record Mom is challenging Rebecca's petition. In line 13, Mom objected to Rebecca as guardian. In line 14, Mom demanded the return of 11,000 from Rebecca.

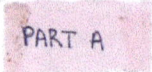

VIRGINIA:

IN THE CIRCUIT COURT FOR THE CITY OF ALEXANDRIA

REBECCA M. WRIGHT,　　　　　　　　　)
　　　　　　　Petitioner,　　　　　　　　　　)
　　　　　　　　　　　　　　　　　　　　　　)
v.　　　　　　　　　　　　　　　　　　　　)　　Case No. CW1100-1267
　　　　　　　　　　　　　　　　　　　　　　)
EDITH HILL,　　　　　　　　　　　　　　　)
　　　　　　　Respondent.　　　　　　　　　)

RESPONSE AND OPPOSITION TO PETITION FOR APPOINTMENT OF GUARDIAN AND CONSERVATOR

COMES NOW the respondent, Edith Hill, by counsel, and for her response and opposition to Petition for Appointment of Guardian and Conservator avers the following:

1. The allegations of paragraph 1 are admitted, except that Petitioner's residence is in Florida.

2. The allegations of paragraph 2 are admitted, except that Respondent is 92 years old (Respondent will be 93 on July 16).

3. With respect to paragraph 3, the allegations are admitted except that Respondent's daughter's real name is Ernestine Yates, not Christina Rosenberg; and that Patricia Cullens Barbour's address is　　　　　　　　　　FL　.

3. With respect to the second numbered paragraph 3, Respondent admits she has been treated by Dr. Ambrish Gupta and that she does not have an Advanced Medical Directive. In all other respects, the allegations of that paragraph are denied.

4. Respondent is without sufficient information to admit or deny the allegations contained in paragraph 4.

5. With respect to paragraph 5, Respondent denies that she has an Arlington Federal Credit Union account as that account was closed by Petitioner. Respondent admits the remaining allegations of paragraph 5, except that her monthly Social Security payment is approximately $1300. Respondent

6. Respondent admits the allegations of paragraph 6, except that her daughter's real name is Ernestine Yates, not Christina Rosenberg and that Patricia Cullens Barbour's address is   Florida

7. The petition omits paragraph 7.

8. Respondent denies the allegations contained in paragraph 8 and demands strict proof thereof.

9. With respect to paragraph 9, Respondent denies that she is incapable of receiving and evaluating information effectively. Respondent admits that she requires some third-party assistance, and affirmatively asserts that she is receiving such assistance from her son, Lewis McDaniel, and has received such assistance from Mr. McDaniel for approximately four years now. In all other respects, the allegations contained in paragraph 9 of the Petition are denied.

10. With respect to paragraph 10, Respondent denies that she is incapable of receiving and evaluating information effectively or responding to people, events, or environments; or that she lacks the capacity to meet essential requirements for her health, care, safety or therapeutic needs without the assistance of a guardian. Respondent affirmatively avers that to the extent she requires assistance with such tasks, she receives such assistance from her son, Lewis McDaniel, and has received such assistance from Mr. McDaniel.

11. Respondent denies the allegations contained in paragraph 11 of the Petition.

12. Respondent affirmatively avers that she is not incapacitated; that she does not require assistance to handle average daily living skills, can manage her finances and personal business affairs with the assistance she now has; and can meet essential requirements for her own health, care, safety, or therapeutic needs. As such, the appointment of a Guardian and Conservator is not necessary and is unwarranted.

13. Should the Court disagree and find that the appointment of a Guardian and Conservator is warranted, Respondent objects to the appointment of her daughter, Rebecca Wright, as the Guardian.

14. Petitioner, unbeknownst to Respondent and without Respondent's authorization or approval, depleted Respondent's bank accounts of at least $11,000. Respondent has demanded the return of those funds, but Petitioner has failed to return those funds. Due, among other things, to such removal of Respondent's monies, Respondent strenuously objects to the appointment of Petitioner as a fiduciary over any property or estate of Respondent.

15. Respondent presently lives with her son, Lewis McDaniel. To the extent that a Guardian and Conservator should be appointed over Respondent's estate, Lewis McDaniel is the proper person for such appointment. Mr. McDaniel presently assists Respondent with certain daily tasks and her financial matters; is aware of Respondent's estate; and is willing to act as Guardian and Conservator.

WHEREFORE, Respondent requests that the Court conduct an evidentiary hearing to determine whether Respondent is incapacitated; that the Court dismiss

Petitioner's Petition For Appointment of Guardian and Conservator, or in the alternative, appoint Respondent's son, Lewis McDaniel, as the Guardian and Conservator of Respondent's estate; and award to Respondent all such other relief as the Court deems just.

EDITH HILL

By: _____
Jeffrey A. Vogelman (VSB No. 19755)
Ciara A. Miller (VSB No. 45661)
Matthew J. Ling (VSB No. 78752)
THOMAS, BALLENGER, VOGELMAN
& TURNER, PC
Street
Alexandria, Virginia
Telephone: (703) 836.
Facsimile: (703) 836.
Her Attorneys

CERTIFICATE OF SERVICE

I hereby certify that a true copy of the foregoing was served this 11th day of July, 2011, upon the following by first-class mail, postage prepaid:

James A. DeVita, Esq.
Blvd., Suite
VA   (and also by facsimile to 703.351.   )

Lewis McDaniel

Alexandria, VA

4

Ernestine Yates

Patricia Barber

Curtis Hubbard

Kenneth E. Labowitz, Esq.
Dingman Labowitz, P.C.
Street, Suite
Alexandria, VA

Jeffrey A. Vogelman

Document 6
Second Answer by guardian AD Litem

In line 5, Ernestine (Tina) is recommended to be guardian and conservator. In line 6, Rebecca admits to Mom's money in her possession.

VIRGINIA:
IN THE CIRCUIT COURT OF THE CITY OF ALEXANDRIA

IN RE: EDITH HILL   ) Fiduciary No. CW11001379
  A person alleged to be incapacitated.   ) Aug. 2, 2011 @ 10:00 a.m.

SECOND ANSWER BY GUARDIAN AD LITEM

COMES NOW, Joshua E. Bushman, duly appointed Guardian ad Litem for EDITH HILL, and for his Second Answer to the Petition for Appointment of Guardianship and Conservatorship pursuant to § 37.2-1000, et seq. of the Code of Virginia, as amended, hereby states the following:

1. Your Guardian ad Litem incorporates by reference all of his previously filed answers in this matter.

2. That this Court has proper jurisdiction over EDITH HILL since she is a resident in the City of Alexandria, Virginia. EDITH HILL is a ninety-two (92) year old woman whose residence is located at   Alexandria, Virginia

3. On July 13, 2011, Complaint, CW11001267, a competing guardianship and conservatorship, filed by Rebecca Wright, by counsel, who is one of the Respondent's daughters was dismissed; thus, leaving this case as the sole petition for appointment of a guardian and conservator

4. Jeffery Vogelman has entered an appearance on behalf of the Respondent, her son, Lewis McDaniel, and one of Respondent's daughters, a proposed guardian and conservator, Ernestine Yates. Rebecca Wright is no longer represented by Mr. Devita.

5. Your Guardian ad Litem spoke with Counsel for Lewis McDaniel, Ernestine Yates, and the respondent. They agree that if a guardianship and conservatorship is necessary

than Ernestine Yates should be the Guardian and Conservator.

6. Your Guardian ad Litem spoke with Rebecca Wright a previous petitioner and one of three daughters of the Respondent. Ms. Wright stated that she is not contesting this matter any further, agrees to the necessity of a guardian and conservator, and that it was her belief that her older sister, Ernestine Yates, would be guardian and conservator. Moreover, she feels that the money in her possession that belongs to the Respondent is rightfully in her possession. It is her position that her mother went to the bank with her and made the transfer knowingly and willingly; furthermore, she stated that other family members could support that contention. Your Guardian ad Litem has not confirmed the veracity of this position by any family members.

7. Your Guardian ad Litem spoke with Patricia Barber, the only other daughter of the Respondent. Ms. Barber agrees with the appointment of Ernestine Yates as the Guardian and Conservator and agrees with the necessity of a guardian and conservator. Furthermore, Your Guardian ad Litem spoke with Curtis Hubbard, brother of the Respondent. Mr. Hubbard supports the appointment of Ernestine Yates.

8. Your Guardian ad Litem was unable to reach Edna Washington, the only sister of the Respondent.

9. Your Guardian ad Litem spoke with counsel for the City of Alexandria, Kenneth Labowitz. It is the City's position that it supports Ernestine Yates as the Guardian and Conservator.

10. Your Guardian ad Litem feels that a Guardian and Conservator of EDITH HILL is necessary, since she cannot adequately care for herself, make her own medical decisions, or

handle her finances.

11. Your Guardian ad Litem recommends the appointment of Ernestine Yates as Guardian and Conservator. However, with the limitation that the power to sell real estate shall be reserved and exercised only after first obtaining court approval.

12. It is recommended that the Respondent continue to receive the services in place and that the guardian pursue other alternatives and options as the Respondent's condition progresses.

13. That a bond in the amount of $1,000.00 without surety is recommended for the Guardian.

14. That a bond in the amount of $50,000.00 with surety is recommended for the Conservator.

15. After full investigation into said Petition, your Guardian ad Litem confirms as true and accurate the allegations contained therein.

WHEREFORE, having Answered the Petitions previously exhibited against EDITH HILL, your Guardian ad Litem submits her interests to the Court and asks that no Decree be entered to her prejudice.

Joshua E. Bushman
Guardian Ad Litem for
EDITH HILL
VSB number 74729
Road, suite
Arlington, Virginia
(703) 524-
(703) 845- Facsimile

Certificate of Service

I do hereby certify that a true and accurate copy of the foregoing Answer by Guardian Ad Litem was transmitted via facsimile and or mailed, first class mail, postage prepaid, this 29 day of July, 2011, to:

Kenneth E. Labowitz
Anne Heishman
Dingman Labowitz, P.C.
　　Street, Suite
Post Office Box
Alexandria, Virginia

Lewis McDaniel

Ernestine Yates

Rebecca Wright

Patricia Barber

Curtis Hubbard

_____
Joshua E. Bushman.
Guardian ad Litem for
EDITH HILL

Document 7
Letter from Law Office

Letter to Rebecca from Ernestine's (Tina's) attorney. It states that Mom is confused, disoriented, agitated, and uneasy when she returns from a visit with Rebecca.

LAW OFFICES
THOMAS, BALLENGER, VOGELMAN AND TURNER, P.C.

ALEXANDRIA, VIRGINIA
(703) 836-
FAX: (703) 836

EARL G. THOMAS (RET.)
JOHN M. BALLENGER (1947-2005)
JEFFREY A. VOGELMAN*
JAMES D. TURNER*

CIARA A. MILLER
MATTHEW J. LING

* VA, GA BARS
* VA, NY, DC BARS

July 2, 2012

Rebecca Wright
        Drive
   Florida

                Road
   Virginia

Re: Edith Hill

Dear Ms. Wright:

       Our office represents Ernestine Yates, as Guardian and Conservator of Edith Hill. Ms. Yates advises me that you have taken Edith Hill on various outings recently. Ms. Yates further advises that Ms. Hill's demeanor is much different after returning from the visit than just prior to her visit with you. Ms. Hill is typically quite calm and content when she leaves with you; however, she returns confused, disoriented, agitated and uneasy. For example, on a recent occasion, Ms. Hill returned from the visit with you and was repeatedly demanding the return of her car (she did not remember agreeing to sell you the car). Due to these problems, Ms. Yates feels that it is in Ms. Hill's best interest that all further visits with you be supervised. In addition, you will no longer be permitted to have overnight visits with Ms. Hill (i.e., visits in which you keep her overnight). All such visitation will need to be arranged with Ms. Yates in advance to ensure that someone is present to supervise the visit.

       On a related note, Ms. Yates advises that Ms. Hill's real property located at Street, Alexandria, Virginia is now vacant. Ms. Yates is looking into either selling or renting the property to generate income for Ms. Hill. She further advises that you may have items of property in the home. Please be advised that you are to remove all items of your tangible personal property on or before July 15, 2012. Any items remaining after that date will be disposed.

                                                       Very truly yours,

                                                         Ciara Miller
                                                         Attorney for Ernestine Yates

Document 8
Care Assessment

On page 5, the Certified Care Manager records her assessment of each sibling's intentions regarding their mother.

CARE ASSESSMENT
Date: December 17, 2013
Client: Mrs. Edith Hill
Completed by:
Kate Caldwell, MA, CMC
Gerontologist and Certified Care Manager

Overview

Mrs. Edith Hill is a 95-year-old woman who currently resides at ███████ Lane, Baltimore, MD ███ with Ernestine Yates, her eldest daughter. My visit was completed at the home on Tuesday, December 17, 2013 at noon. The guardian ad litem, Mr. Joshua E. Bushman, accompanied me. Also present was Ms. Eunell Marshall, Certified Nursing Assistant. I was first contacted by Mr. Bushman about an assessment of activities of daily living for Mrs. Hill, then later contacted by Pirsch and Associates to confirm that all parties involved agreed that an assessment take place.

Medical/Health

Mrs. Hill was born July 16, 1918. Her primary care physician is Dr. Ambrish Gupta in Alexandria, VA. Ms. Yates has been caring for her mother in her home since November 2011. Ms. Yates shared little of her mother's medical history, stating her mother had very few problems and was in no pain. Ms. Yates did share that in 2011 her mother was diagnosed with breast cancer and she suffers from an unknown cause of dementia. According to Ms. Yates, Mrs. Hill is over due to see Dr. Gupta, as they missed her last appointment.

Mrs. Hill was able to ambulate with stand-by assistance; she was somewhat unsteady on her feet although does not use a cane or walker. She was also able to ambulate down the stairs with close stand-by assistance. Mrs. Hill was not wearing glasses during our meeting. Ms. Yates reported that her mother only wears glasses for nearsightedness. Mrs. Hill had no issues hearing me and answered my questions appropriately. She was well dressed and well groomed. Mrs. Hill's fingernails and toenails were nicely painted, although she would benefit from a podiatrist, as her toenails were sharp and cracked. The Certified Nursing Assistant (CNA), Ms. Eunell Marshall, stated that Mrs. Hill takes showers and uses lotion daily. I suggested cutting this back to a few times a week, as Mrs. Hill's skin was very dry. Ms. Marshall also stated that Mrs. Hill is continent of bowel and bladder and uses the bathroom throughout the day. At night she has a portable

ElderTree Care Management Services
www.ElderTreecare.com/ 703-424-████ Office

commode next to the bed. Ms. Yates sleeps on the same floor as her mother to assist her if necessary at night.

According to both Ms. Yates and Ms. Marshall, Mrs. Hill has been very sleepy and takes frequent rests, especially after she eats a meal. Ms. Yates is concerned about her mother's lack of energy and explained to Mr. Bushman and me that this is the reason why she does not take her mother out much and why Mrs. Hill no longer attends the adult day center. Mrs. Hill sleeps through the night without any issues. Mrs. Hill does get out to the hairdresser and to the doctor's office as long as Ms. Yates has assistance from the CNA to do so.

Diagnoses Noted During Visit:

Breast Cancer diagnosed in November 2012
Mild Progressive Dementia (cause unknown) diagnosed in 2011 by Dr. Gupta
Hypertension
Osteopenia
Constipation

Current Medication list:

Medication	Dose	Reason	Physician
Namenda	10 MG	Dementia	Dr. Gupta
Letrozole	2.5MG	Breast Cancer	Dr. Couzi
Losartan HCTZ	100/25 MG	Hypertension	Dr. Gupta
Colace	100mg /as needed	Constipation	Dr. Gupta
Vitamin D3			
Multivitamin			

Current Physicians

Dr. Ambrish K. Gupta Primary Care Physician	Duke St. Ste Alexandria, VA	Phone: (703) 658- Fax:
Dr. Rima J. Couzi Oncologist	Osler Dr. Ste Towson, MD	Phone: (410) 427- Fax:

Current Living Environment:

Mrs. Hill lives with her daughter, Ms. Yates, in a three-level town home. The home was clean and orderly when we arrived. Mrs. Hill spends time in her room, in her own kitchen, in the living room, and in the family kitchen. I would recommend a physical

ElderTree Care Management Services
www.ElderTreecare.com/ 703-424-   Office

therapist come to the home for a home safety evaluation and for strength training to prevent falls.

Nutrition/Hydration:

Mrs. Hill currently weighs 112 pounds and reported having a good appetite. According to Mrs. Hill and her daughter, she has always had a slender frame. While Mr. Bushman and I were present she ate a full lunch. Mrs. Hill has dentures that are loose; I would recommend she see a prosthodontist, a dentist who specializes in dentures. Mrs. Hill drinks fluids throughout the day with no issues swallowing, and does not appear dehydrated. According to Ms. Yates, she is not able to tolerate nutritional shakes like Boost or Ensure.

Needs Assessment:

Based on the data we gathered, the following are Mrs. Hill's caregiving needs at this time:

Activities of Daily Living: Mrs. Hill requires some assistance with all activities of daily living.

Eating	reminders only (mechanical soft consistency)
Ambulation	unsteady gait/ stand-by assistance
Transfers	one person stand-by assistance
Bathing	stand-by and hands-on assistance
Dressing	stand-by and hands-on assistance
Grooming	stand-by assistance and cueing
Toileting	on a schedule/is continent, needs assistance in bathroom

Instrumental Activities of Daily Living: Mrs. Hill is dependent on her daughter and the CNA to have these activities met on a daily basis.

Meal Preparation	dependent
Shopping	dependent
Laundry	dependent
Medical Coordination	dependent
Medication Management	dependent
Transportation	dependent

Socialization/Mood:

According to Ms. Yates, her mother has been too tired to go on outings. Mrs. Hill enjoys going to church, and sang in a choir for many years. According to Ms. Yates, she now becomes too exhausted when she goes to church. Mrs. Hill's boyfriend of   years, Mr. Eddie Harrison, lives in Alexandria. He calls daily and they talk on the phone. From what we observed during our visit, Mrs. Hill and her daughter seem to have a positive relationship. When I asked Mrs. Hill if she was happy, she expressed her sadness and grief over losing her son to leukemia in 2012. She seemed content and cared for in her daughter's home. According to Ms. Yates, Mrs. Hill is never left at home alone.

Summary and Recommendations:

Mrs. Hill lives with her daughter, Ms. Ernestine Yates, who has been her primary caregiver since November 2011. A Certified Nursing Assistant comes to the home on average five days per week to assist Ms. Yates and give her some respite to run errands. Mrs. Hill appears to be in excellent physical shape for her age and well cared for. Although I feel Ms. Yates is doing her best to care for her mother, I have a few recommendations below.

My recommendations for Mrs. Hill's current needs are the following:

- Schedule an appointment for Mrs. Hill to see a podiatrist for her cracked toenails.
- Limit bathing to two or three times a week to prevent dry skin.
- If it should become too difficult for Mrs. Hill to see Dr. Gupta in Alexandria, find a physician in the Baltimore area, possibly even one who will do home visits.
- Schedule an appointment for Mrs. Hill to see a dentist who specializes in dentures, as hers are loose.
- Schedule a home safety evaluation and physical therapy evaluation by a home health agency.
- Hire a Certified Nursing Assistant through a reputable agency rather than privately.
- Secure Mrs. Hill's medication in a lock box. While she is not on many medications, this could prevent an accident.
- Create an emergency folder with an updated medication list, current diagnoses, legal documents, and wishes. The CNA should know the location of this folder and there should be a copy in the car.

Phone interview with Ms. Patricia Barber

On January 13, 2014, Kate Caldwell and Ms. Cary Cucinelli of the Ruddy Law Firm held a conference call with Ms. Patricia Barber. Ms. Barber provided a wealth of information on her mother's medical history. She shared her concerns about Ms. Yates' ability to care for her mother and wishes to care for her mother in her home in Florida. Ms. Barber felt strongly that her mother would be best cared-for in her home with family around at all times (there is a large support system). Ms. Barber has a plan of care in place; she does not want her mother to be placed in a facility.

Phone call with Ms. Ernestine Yates

On January 24, 2014, Kate Caldwell received a call from Ms. Yates about paying her invoice. She stated that she had called a Place for Mom, as she was considering placing her mother in a facility in Baltimore.

Interview with Ms. Rebecca McDaniel Wright

On January 29, 2014, Kate Caldwell and Ms. Ena Richter of Pirsch and Associates met with Rebecca Wright. Ms. Wright spoke passionately about caring for her mother and her goal to be appointed Guardian and move her mother back to her home in Alexandria. She would like to provide her mother a loving, safe and predictable environment in her own home. She shared her many concerns about the care Ms. Yates is providing her mother and her feeling that when Mr. Bushman and I made our assessment, Ms. Yates staged the visit. Ms. Wright has a plan of care for her mother, although it is based on residing in the family home, of which the condition is unknown. When asked, she made it clear that her mother would never want to move to an assisted living community.

Report prepared and submitted by:
Kate H. Caldwell, MA, CMC

Founder ElderTree Care Management
ElderTree Care Management Services
www.ElderTreecare.com / 703-424-   Office

Document 9
Court Order

*Original handwritten agreement. All parties and attorneys were present in court and agreed to remove Ernestine (Tina) as guardian and conservator. The official typed agreement was delivered at a later date. Line 8 states that Mom lacks the legal capacity to enter into contracts that would bind her estate. Line 13 provides that the co-conservators are **prohibited from selling her real property.***

VIRGINIA:

IN THE CIRCUIT COURT FOR THE CITY OF ALEXANDRIA

In Re: Estate of Edith Hill

~~Plaintiff~~

vs.   Case Number CW 11001379

~~Defendant~~

ORDER

This cause came on this day upon Rebecca Wright by Counsel, Patricia Barber by Counsel, Ernestine Yates by Counsel, & Joshua E. Bushman

AND IT APPEARING that the parties having reached an agreement (competing) on all petitions & motions set for a hearing on February 24, 2014;

It is therefore

ORDERED, ADJUDGED, AND DECREED that Ernestine Yates' appointment as Guardian & Conservator is vacated, and shall file a final accounting within four months or as agreed with the Commissioner of Accounts. Patricia E. Barber and Rebecca M. Wright as Co-Guardians and Co-Conservators. Bond for the Co-Guardians shall be $1,000 without surety and & Conservators. or Attached Sheet #1

ENTERED this 24 day of February, 2014

_____
James C. Clark, Judge

SEEN: SEEN & AGREED:

_____   _____
Counsel for the ~~Plaintiff~~ Petitioner   Counsel for ~~Defendant~~ Petitioner, Rebecca Wright

CARYL CUNELLI   Albany (VSB 83317)
COUNSEL TO
PATRICIA
BARBER
#72107   Joshua E. Bushman as
           Guardian ad Litem, VSB #74729

Attached Sheet #1

Furthermore Ordered that the Co-Conservators shall post a bond of $30,000.00 with surety.

Furthermore Ordered that Rebecca M. Wright shall have physical custody of Edith Hill from entry of this order until March 12, 2014. Rebecca M. Wright shall transfer physical custody to Patricia E. Barber in Florida, on March 12, 2014 at 12 p.m. Patricia E. Barber shall have physical custody until the Renovations are complete to return Edith Hill to her home at ____ St.

Furthermore Ordered that the parties will enter an order governing more definite terms such as those needed by the Co-guardians & Co-conservators as Representative Payee or Authorized agent under H.I.P.P.A. as Amended. Any repairs shall be guided by a geriatric care manager or a neutral 3rd party as chosen and agreed by the Co-Guardians. The Amended order shall be submitted to the court by March 12, 2014.

Seen & Agreed   Seen & Agreed   Seen USB #19755

Rebecca M. Wright   _Patricia Barber_   _Jeffrey A. Vogelin_
REBECCA M. WRIGHT   PATRICIA BARBER   Attorney for Franklin Yale

VIRGINIA:

IN THE CIRCUIT COURT FOR THE CITY OF ALEXANDRIA

IN RE: ESTATE OF EDITH HILL   Case No.: CW11001379

ORDER

THIS CAUSE came to be heard on the 28th day of May, 2014, upon the Petitions of Rayfield Barber and Patricia Barber, son-in-law and daughter of Edith Hill; Rebecca Wright, daughter of Edith Hill; and Ernestine Yates, daughter of Edith Hill, with appearances by Cary Z. Cucinelli, Counsel for petitioners Rayfield Barber and Patricia Barber; Ena Richter, Counsel for petitioner Rebecca Wright; and Joshua B. Bushman, Guardian ad litem;

AND IT APPEARING that the parties reached agreement on all competing petitions and motions which were set for hearing on February 24, 2014, and an interim order, the terms of which are incorporated herein, was entered on that day, with the expectation that an amended order would be submitted soon thereafter; it is therefore

ADJUDGED, ORDERED AND DECREED as follows:

1. Ernestine Yates' appointment as Guardian and Conservator is vacated and Ernestine Yates shall file a final accounting no later than June 24, 2014 or as agreed with the Commissioner of Accounts.

2. Patricia E. Barber and Rebecca M. Wright are appointed as Co-Guardians of Edith Hill with all powers and duties granted to a Guardian pursuant to §64.2-2019 of the Code of Virginia. The Co-Guardians shall be required to post a personal bond without surety in the amount of $1,000 and make reports as required by §64.2-2020 of the Code of Virginia.

3. Rebecca M. Wright shall have physical custody of Edith Hill from entry of this

order until March 12, 2014. Rebecca M. Wright shall transfer physical custody to Patricia E. Barber on March 12, 2014, at 12:00 pm in ⎯⎯⎯⎯ Florida. Patricia E. Barber shall thereafter have physical custody of Edith Hill, until the required renovations (hereinafter defined) to ⎯⎯⎯⎯ Street in Alexandria, Virginia, are complete and the completion is confirmed by a professional geriatric care manager, as described below. The "required renovations" are all repairs, restorations, and renovations necessary to ensure that ⎯⎯⎯⎯ in Alexandria, Virginia, is a safe, habitable, and comfortable home in which Edith Hill may reside. Whether the required renovations are complete shall be determined by a professional geriatric care manager selected by both Co-Guardians; if the Co-Guardians cannot agree on the selection of a professional geriatric care manager, then Joshua B. Bushman, Esq. shall select a professional geriatric care manager.

4. The "required renovations" described herein shall be paid for by Rebecca M. Wright from her own funds. While the Estate of Edith Hill shall not be responsible for reimbursing Rebecca M. Wright for the costs, during Edith Hill's life, Rebecca M. Wright may seek reimbursement of those costs from the future sale of ⎯⎯⎯⎯ in Alexandria, Virginia. Likewise, the costs of the professional geriatric care manager's assessment of the required renovations' completion shall be paid for from Rebecca M. Wright's own funds.

5. Patricia E. Barber and Rebecca M. Wright are hereby appointed as Co-Conservators of Edith Hill with all powers and duties granted to a Conservator pursuant to §64.2-2021 et seq. of the Code of Virginia and with all powers set forth in §64.2-105 of the Code of Virginia. The Co-Conservators shall be required to post a bond with a licensed surety in the amount of $30,000.

6. Each Co-Conservator may act unilaterally and without the consent of the other Co-Conservator with respect to Edith Hill's bank accounts such that any and all banking institutions may deal with either Co-Conservator, should not require both Co-Conservators' signatures on checks and other transactions related to Edith Hill's accounts, and shall be entitled to rely upon the instructions of one Co-Conservator.

7. In compliance with the Health Insurance Portability and Accountability Act of 1996 (HIPAA), Co-Guardians Patricia E. Barber and Rebecca M. Wright shall be considered the "personal representative" for health care disclosures under HIPAA with the same access to Protected Health Information (PHI) as Edith Hill would have.

8. The legal disabilities of Edith Hill are total and complete with respect to her person and to her estate as defined in §64.2-2000 of the Code of Virginia and Edith Hill shall have no power with respect to her estate as so defined, and she shall be legally incapable of entering into any contract to bind or convey her estate, or to make any inter vivos gift of any portion of her estate, or of owning or possessing any firearm.

9. That this adjudication of incapacity is also a finding that Edith Hill is "incompetent" for purposes of the Social Security Act, particularly with reference to the appointment of a representative payee for Social Security or other governmental benefits due to her, as the term "incompetent" is defined under 20 Code of Federal Regulations §404.2015.

10. The driving license and driving privileges of Edith Hill are hereby revoked.

11. This Order shall not abridge Edith Hill's right to vote.

12. Any powers of attorney granted by Edith Hill to any person are hereby revoked and canceled.

13. The Co-Conservators do not have power of sale to sell and convey the real property of Edith Hill.

14. Pursuant to §64.2-2003 of the Code of Virginia, Guardian ad litem Joshua Bushman, Esq., shall be paid a fee of $6,575, in addition to the $3,713.56 owed him, pursuant to this Court's order of August 2, 2011. The fees shall be paid from the estate of Edith Hill, said amount to be a lien against real property owned by Edith Hill with interest at the judgment rate from the date of this Order. It is the intention of the Court that the award made to Mr. Bushman shall be paid from the sale or transfer of the title to real property owned by Ms. Hill. Joshua Bushman, Esq. is discharged from further responsibility in this matter.

ENTERED this 2Y day of May, 2014.

JUDGE

A COPY TESTE:
EDWARD SEMONIAN, CLERK
BY _____, DEPUTY CLERK
CERTIFIED THIS 23th DAY OF May, 2014

SEEN _____:

_____
Jeffrey A. Vogelman, VSB No. 19755
Thomas, Ballenger, Vogelman, & Turner, P.C.
          Street
Alexandria, VA
jvogelman@   .com
Counsel to Rayfield Barber and Patricia Barber Ernestine Yates

SEEN _____:

_____
Ena Juvardo Richter, VSB No. 83397
Pirsch & Associates, PLLC
          Street
Alexandria, VA
ena@   .net
Counsel to Rebecca M. Wright

SEEN _Agreed_____:

[signature]
Joshua Bushman, VSB No. 74729
Bushman Law Group
          Road, Suite
Arlington, VA
josh.bushman@   .com
Guardian ad Litem for Edith Hill

SEEN _and agreed_____:

[signature]
Cary Z. Cucinelli, VSB No. 72102
The Ruddy Law Firm
          Street, Suite
Fairfax, Virginia
703-383-   ext. / 703-383-   (fax)
ccucinelli@   .com
Counsel to Rayfield Barber and Patricia E. Barber

Document 10
Florida Cancer Specialists

This list reflects a portion of Mom's medical appointments, with the final row indicating the anticipated time frame for her return to Florida. Rebecca did not willingly return Mom after the April 14th appointment.

OncoEMR-Visit List

[Options] [Close]

Florida Cancer Specialists - Memorial Medical - Dr. Ndum
Parkway
Suite
Florida
Phone: (386)586-   Fax: 855-774-

Visit List for Edith Hill
For the Memorial Medical-Dr. Ndum office only

Date	Time	Location	Plan
Friday, April 11, 2014	10:00 AM	Memorial Medical-Dr. Ndum	Visit with Philip Ndum MD
Monday, April 14, 2014		Memorial Medical-Dr. Ndum	Radiology: Mammogram-diagnostic, Ultrasound Breast
Thursday, July 31, 2014	1:30 PM	Memorial Medical-Dr. Ndum	Visit with Ndum

https://onco2.flcancer.com/pages pd/PD VisitsOnDate.aspx?WHAT=L& OS=GH 0818... 4/11/2014

Document 11
Petition for removal of co-guardian and co-conservator and appointment of standby guardian and conservator

This document outlines several instances in which Rebecca failed to act in Mom's best interest.

PART C

VIRGINIA:

IN THE CIRCUIT COURT OF CITY OF ALEXANDRIA

In Re: Estate of Edith Hill) Fiduciary Case No.: CW11001379
)
)

**PETITION FOR REMOVAL OF CO-GUARDIAN AND CO-CONSERVATOR
AND APPOINTMENT OF STANDBY GUARDIAN AND CONSERVATOR**

COMES NOW, PATRICIA BARBER ("Petitioner"), Co-Guardian and Co-Conservator of EDITH HILL, by and through counsel, to petition this Court to remove REBECCA M. WRIGHT ("Respondent") as Co-Guardian and Co-Conservator of EDITH HILL, appoint Petitioner as sole Guardian and Conservator and Petitioner's husband, RAYFIELD BARBER, as standby Guardian and Conservator. In support of said petition, Petitioner states as follows:

1. This is a proceeding brought under the provisions of Va. Code Sections 64.2-2012 and 64.2-2021 et seq.

2. Pursuant to Va. Code Section 64.2-2012, this Court may award appropriate relief upon finding by a preponderance of evidence that the Guardian and Conservator is not acting in the best interests of the incapacitated person or of her estate.

3. On February 24, 2014, Petitioner and Respondent were appointed by this Court as Co-Guardian and Co-Conservator of their mother, EDITH HILL.

4. Since the sisters' appointment as co-fiduciaries for their mother, Ms. Wright has attempted to circumvent the Court system, avoided her responsibilities as Co-Guardian and Co-Conservator, and failed to communicate with Petitioner.

5. Respondent is not acting in the best interests of EDITH HILL and the only appropriate relief that this Court can grant is the removal of Respondent.

6. The orders entered by this Court (copies of which are attached hereto as **Exhibits**

1

A and B) provide that Patricia E. Barber shall have physical custody of Edith Hill, until the required renovations to _____ Street in Alexandria, Virginia, are complete and that the required renovations are to be paid for by Rebecca M. Wright from her own funds.

7. Respondent has reconsidered and now regrets the agreement she made with respect to her mother's residence at _____ Street.

8. In early spring 2014, Petitioner consented to Respondent's request to take Edith Hill from Florida to Virginia for a short trip. As of the date of this petition, Petitioner believes that her mother, Edith Hill, remains in Respondent's custody; however, Respondent is not communicating (not answering Petitioner's phone calls nor returning Petitioner's phone messages) with Petitioner nor other family members. In fact, Respondent's attorney does not know where Respondent is vacationing nor whether Edith Hill is with Respondent.

9. Respondent has failed to seek medical care for Edith Hill. Before traveling to Virginia, Respondent confirmed that she would ensure her mother's receipt of the treatment recommended by her mother's Florida oncologist (from whom permission to travel was received on the promise that the recommended procedure would be completed in Virginia) but has failed to do so.

10. The (partially handwritten) order entered by this Court on February 24, 2014, provides that an order "governing more definite terms" should be submitted to the Court by March 12, 2014. Despite efforts by Petitioner's and Respondent's attorneys to draft an order acceptable to Petitioner and Respondent, Respondent failed to agree to the most basic provisions necessary for inclusion in an order appointing guardians and conservators. Knowing that the failure to have entered the subsequent order would lead to the closure of Edith Hill's only bank

account, Respondent nevertheless advised her attorney to not sign the order required to be submitted and insisted that her attorney not attend the hearing on the matter.

WHEREFORE, Petitioner PATRICIA BARBER prays this Court to do the following:

(1) Remove Respondent REBECCA M. WRIGHT as Co-Guardian and Co-Conservator of Edith Hill;

(2) Appoint Petitioner PATRICIA BARBER sole Guardian and Conservator of Edith Hill;

(3) Appoint Petitioner's husband, RAYFIELD BARBER, standby Guardian and Conservator for of Edith Hill;

(4) Award reasonable attorney's fees and costs to the Petitioner in this matter; and order such other appropriate relief.

Respectfully submitted,

PATRICIA BARBER
By Counsel

Cary Z. Cucinelli, VSB No. 72102
Counsel to Rayfield Barber and Patricia E. Barber
The Ruddy Law Firm
Street, Suite
Fairfax, Virginia
703-383-   ext. 3 / 703-383-   (fax)
ccucinelli@   .com

CERTIFICATE OF SERVICE

This is to certify that, on this 17th day of June, 2014, a true and exact copy of the foregoing Petition was sent by electronic mail and mailed U.S. Mail, first-class postage prepaid, to:

Joshua Bushman, Esq.
The Bushman Law Group
              Road, Suite
Arlington, VA

Jeffrey A. Vogelman, Esq.
Thomas, Ballenger, Vogelman & Turner, P.C.
              Street
Alexandria, VA

Ena Richter, Esq.
Pirsch & Associates, PLLC
              Street
Alexandria, VA

Rayfield & Patricia Barber
              Place
              FL

_____
Cary Z. Cucinelli

Document 12
Care Assessment

This report was requested by Jessica Niesen, the new court appointed guardian. Due to the lack of agreement between us siblings, our positions were subsequently vacated. The report highlights several addresses that Rebecca used to evade and manipulate contact. It also references filming that took place and expresses the care manager's doubt regarding Rebecca's ability to adequately care for Mom.

CARE ASSESSMENT
Date: October 17th 2014
Client: Mrs. Edith Hill
Completed by: Kate Caldwell, MA, CMC

Overview

Mrs. Edith Hill is a 96-year-old woman who currently resides with her daughter Ms. Rebecca McDaniel Wright and Mrs. Hill's newlywed husband (June 21st 2014) Mr. Eddie Harrison, also in his 90's. They reside mainly at Ms. Wright's home located at   Street, Annandale, VA   They spend a lot of time at Rebecca's lake house   Farmhand, VA   (approximately 2 hours drive), and most recently they spend time at   St. Alexandria VA, Mrs. Hill's home. I last met with Mrs. Hill December 17th 2013 when she resided at   Lane, Baltimore, MD   with Ernestine Yates, her eldest daughter. I have been requested to assess Mrs. Hill by her Guardian Ms. Jessica Niesen, Attorney at Law. My current role is to complete a comprehensive care assessment for Mrs. Edith Hill. This will include her current level of care needs and recommendations on the appropriate living environment.

My first attempt to see Mrs. Hill was on September 18th when arrangements were made with Ms. Wright to meet at the   St. home. When I arrived Ms. Robin Wright Mrs. Hill's granddaughter was at the home and stated the meeting was to be at the   St. House. Ms. Rebecca Wright stated on the phone that the camera crew was there to film the assessment. I asked to reschedule the meeting, as the Guardian would need to give permission for video taping Mrs. Hill at any time.

My second attempt to see Mrs. Hill was October 17th at the   St. House. I met with Mrs. Hill, Rebecca Wright, and a cousin Laurie. Mr. Harrison was sleeping though out the visit in the upstairs bedroom, it was reported that he was not feeling well. The following report details the information from this October meeting.

Medical/Health

Mrs. Hill was born July 16, 1918. Her primary care physician is Dr. Ambrish Gupta in Alexandria, VA. I have reviewed the most recent medical records from this group to find her last appointment was August 20th 2014. An Echocardiogram was performed. There was no note of any changes in her plan of care.

ElderTree Care Management Services
www.ElderTreecare.com/ 703-424-   Office

In 2011 Mrs. Hill was diagnosed with breast cancer. I have reviewed the most recent medical records from Dr. Ivan Aksentijevich with Virginia Cancer Specialist. The last appointment was on May 21st 2014. Dr. Aksentijevich reports that Mrs. Hill has tolerated her treatment well and that she "has no palpable disease today" meaning he cannot feel the cancer by touch. The doctor notes that he is not going to recommend any changes at this time and states that Ms. Wright agrees with this current plan of care. Dr. Aksentijevich did recommend calcium, vitamin D, and Fosamax. The report stated there was a mammogram completed 4/2014 although no note as to the results of this procedure. I reported to Ms. Wright that the Guardian stated a follow-up appointment was scheduled for November 6th at 11AM. Ms. Wright wanted to know who made the appointment. Ms. Wright said her mother is supposed to see Dr. Aksentijevich in October and she will make the appointment.

Ms. Wright reported that her mother went to see Dr. Gupta two weeks ago. She also stated that her mother is no longer on her medications except for the Letrozole, for breast cancer. I asked if Dr. Gupta was aware of this and she said yes. Upon showing Rebecca the former list of medication she stated that her mother still takes the vitamin D and the multivitamin. This report from Ms. Wright is not reflected in Dr. Gupta's records. According to Dr. Gupta the last visit was August 20th 2014 and there were no medication changes noted at the time of the appointment.

Mrs. Hill was able to ambulate on the lower level of the home with her cane although her gait was unsteady. She was able to stand up from a seated position with her cane although again she was unsteady. When I met her last December she was not using a cane at that time in the home. With complete stand by assistance she was able to ambulate up the stairs and down the stairs. In December she was able to go up and down the stairs with simple stand by assistance. When I last saw Mrs. Hill she had no issues hearing me and answered my questions in general appropriately. During this visit she was having a very difficult time hearing me and understanding what I was asking her. I suggest she have her hearing tested by an audiologist. Mrs. Hill was well dressed and well groomed. Ms. Wright reported that her mother wears an incontinent pad, especially on long trips, although is otherwise able to get to the bathroom.

According to Ms. Wright both Mrs. Hill and Mr. Harrison sleep in late and also take naps. When asked about their schedule Ms. Wright said they start with breakfast, exercise, listen to music and dance. They enjoy going to JV's nightclub on Wednesday and Sunday and going to church.

ElderTree Care Management Services
www.ElderTreecare.com/ 703-424-   Office

Diagnoses:

Breast Cancer
Mild progressive Dementia (cause unknown)
Hypertension
Osteopenia
Constipation

Current Medication list:

Medication	Dose	Reason	Physician
Namenda	10 MG	Dementia	Dr. Gupta
Letrozole	2.5MG	Breast Cancer	Dr. Aksentijevich
Losartan HCTZ	100/25 MG	Hypertension	Dr. Gupta
Colace	100mg /as needed	Constipation	Dr. Gupta
Fosamax	Recommended by:		Dr. Aksentijevich
Calcium	Recommended by:		Dr. Aksentijevich
Vitamin D3	Recommended by:		Dr. Aksentijevich
Multivitamin			

Current Physicians

Dr. Ambrish K. Gupta Primary Care Physician	St. Ste Alexandria, VA	Phone: (703) 658- Fax: (703) 658-
Dr. Ivan Aksentijevich	Ave. # Alexandria, VA	Phone: (571) 438- Fax: (703) 823-

Current Living Environment:

Mrs. Hill lives with her daughter, Rebecca Wright in three different locations. During my visit to the   St. house it was stated that they are all now living there and going to the river house. Rebecca and Laurie have spent time cleaning and de-cluttering the home and refinishing the hard wood floor. The home consists of a TV/living room area, a small dining area, and galley kitchen. There are steep stairs going to the upper level that consists of two small bedrooms and a bathroom with a bathtub/shower. There was a shower bench in the shower. I suggested a hand held showerhead and Ms. Wright felt this was not necessary. I suggested a chair lift and Ms. Wright felt this would not work

ElderTree Care Management Services
www.ElderTreecare.com/ 703-424-   Office

for this home. When I asked Ms. Wright how she is going to get her mother and Mr. Harrison up the stairs to bed and to the bathroom when they decline. She stated she would move their bed down stairs and she would put her mother in a diaper.

Nutrition/Hydration:

Mrs. Hill currently weighs 110 pounds and Ms. Wright reports her mother has a good appetite. She was 112 pounds when I met her last December. Ms. Wright stated that she feeds her mother fish and plenty of fruits and veggies. Mrs. Hill is still wearing her dentures and Ms. Wright uses Fixodent to keep them in place. I had recommended a consult with a Prostondontist in the past to ensure Mrs. Hill's current dentures are fitting properly and I recommend this again.

Needs Assessment:

Based on the data I gathered, the following are Mrs. Hill's caregiving needs at this time:

Activities of Daily Living: Mrs. Hill requires assistance with all activities of daily living, although she is still able to feed herself.

Eating	reminders only
Ambulation	unsteady gait/ stand-by assistance
Transfers	one person stand-by assistance
Bathing	stand-by and hands-on assistance
Dressing	stand-by and hands-on assistance
Grooming	stand-by assistance and cueing
Toileting	on a schedule/is continent, needs assistance in bathroom

Instrumental Activities of Daily Living: Mrs. Hill is dependent on her daughter to have these activities met on a daily basis.

Meal Preparation	dependent
Shopping	dependent
Laundry	dependent
Medical Coordination	dependent
Medication Management	dependent
Transportation	dependent

ElderTree Care Management Services
www.ElderTreecare.com/ 703-424- Office

Socialization/Mood:

According to Ms. Wright, her mother loves to go places and do things. Mrs. Hill enjoys going to church, to the grocery store, and to the Kennedy center. She enjoys helping out around the house doing life skills such as folding laundry and doing dishes. Mrs. Hill loves music and enjoys dancing with Mr. Harrison. Mrs. Wright states that the marriage brings joy to her mother. She states that this is the third marriage for Mrs. Hill and for Mr. Harrison. She explained that Mr. Harrison's late wife had dementia and he is a very skilled caregiver.

Summary and Recommendations:

Mrs. Hill lives with her daughter, Ms. Rebecca Wright with some assistance from her granddaughter Ms. Robin Wright and the cousin Laurie. Although I feel Ms. Wright deeply loves her mother she does not have the nursing skills to be the full-time caregiver for her mother and in addition caring for Mr. Harrison. Ms. Wright has stated a number of times she was planning to take a certified nursing class and she has not followed though on this.

As well, I strongly believe moving Mrs. Hill from house to house is not beneficial for her. In my meeting with Ms. Wright last January, Ms. Wright stated that she would like to provide her mother a loving, safe, and predictable environment in her own home (St). She has not proven this moving her mother from house to house.

My final concern is the exploitation of Mrs. Hill and Mr. Harrison's right to privacy through having interviews with news media and videotaping. The Guardian has requested Ms. Wright stop this and she continues to schedule interviews with discussions of documentaries and movies.

My recommendations for Mrs. Hill's current needs are the following:

- I recommend Mrs. Hill move to an assisted living community in the Alexandria area where she will receive medical oversight, 3 meals a day, and a predictable environment.

- I recommend the family tour the following 3 communities and make a decision as soon as possible. The following 3 communities are selected from a list of assisted communities, which have auxiliary grant beds in the case that Mrs. Hill should run out of resources to pay for assisted living. The goal would be that she would not

need to move although there is no guarantee that a grant bed will be open at the time of need.

1. Sunrise of Alexandria
2. Sunrise of Mt. Vernon
3. Culpepper Garden
4. District Home (Assisted Living)

Report prepared and submitted by:

Kate H. Caldwell

Kate H. Caldwell, MA, CMC
ElderTree Care Management

Document 13
Series of Emails

Emails expressing concerns over Mom's well-being. Rebecca discontinued Mom's medication without proper authorization from her doctors. In addition, the scene of seperation in the documentary was, in fact, a pre-scheduled transfer, as confirmed in the email dated November 20, 2014.

Date: Wed, 19 Nov 2014 16:57:09 -0500
Subject: medication situation update....
From: jjniesen76@   .com
To: pebarber@   .com; flower8740@   .net

So we aren't sure if Rebeccah simply made up the comment or what the scenario was but we've confirmed that Dr. Gupta did not give that instruction and that Rebeccah will bring mom into see him immediately/asap to ensure she is healthy and get the prescriptions refilled. Rebecch told her counsel that it was "scotty" from Dr. Gupta's office that told her that, and Dr. Gupta's office indicates that Scotty is no longer working with them or for them.   Not sure exactly where the truth is but its being corrected.

I have Kate getting the records from the 11/6 visit with the VA Cancer Specialists.

J
--

Jessica J. Niesen
Attorney at Law
Law Offices
703.527.   (office)
703.338.   (cellular)

SCHEDULED FLORIDA VISIT - HILL, EDITH

From: **Jessica Niesen** (jjniesen76@   .com)
Sent: Thu 11/20/14 12:52 PM
To: Chew, Benjamin (BChew@   .com); Kate Caldwell (kate@   .com); Patricia Barber (pebarber@   .com); flower8740@   .net

Hi Ben,

I'm hearing more about bars, night clubs and Casinos, even this week with the bitter cold. Between that, the being in the home that is been labeled as unsafe for her by a Geriatric Care Manager and the medication situation I've made the determination that the time has come to get Edith into a situation that is safer and more stable.

As Edith's Guardian I've granted permission to Patricia Barber to come to Virginia, pick up Edith and return to Florida for a few weeks visit. My intention is to find a placement for her in Virginia in the mean time. Patricia will return with Edith and get her settled into the Assisted Living Home where all her family can come visit her and Eddie in a safe stable environment that can provide her and Eddie with the proper level of skilled care they both require.

As I've always stated I will make these arrangement so that Eddie may accompany Edith if he chooses to. But we are at a standstill and we can no longer afford to wait. We risk Edith's health, welfare and her life at this point.

I expect Rebeccah to have Edith at   Street this weekend to be picked up by Patricia. If she is not there Ill have to consider that Rebeccah has kidnapped Edith as she does not have my permission to have her in any other location.

Please inform your client as to these instructions. I appreciate your continued assistance in effectuating these necessary and very important changes.

I am hopeful that Rebeccah can see the wisdom of this decision and I encourage her to genuinely place her mother's well-being before her personal life choices and feelings about the matter. I'd love to see the family working together to protect and cherish their mother.

I'm cc'ing Kate, Patricia and Ernestine on this email. We'll continue to coordinate in the next few weeks.

Jessica

Mail - pebarber@ .com

RE: medication situation update....

Patricia Barber

Fri 11/21/2014 10:57 AM

To: jjniesen76@ .com <jjniesen76@ .com>;

Jessica,

As we wait for response from Rebecca and/or her council..........

Just to touch base this morning on transition of Mom to Fla. I reached out to family members (Ernestine, Curtis, Lois (granddaughter) including my husband and 2 sons..They all agree that given the history and circumstances surrounding (Rebecca's behavior)...their preference would be to make Mom's transition in a more controlled setting with them being present.

The first week in Dec. for them is a better fit (Curtis is out of town (will be back next week) Ernestine has a cold (next week is better for her)...granddaughter (Lois) is already in the area.

Also this gives Rebecca more time to take Mom to visit Dr. Gupta's office and get the proper medicines as he prescribes or refills the needed medications before she travels....

Grapevine is saying that Rebecca is *filming * this weekend....and with plans to travel for the Thanksgiving holiday....

Document 14
Letter from Elder Care Consultant

The gerontologist is not recommending Mom to travel back home to Virginia.

To whom it may concern,

I was hired as a professional Geriatric Care Manager and Elder Care Consultant by Ms. Jessica Niesen, Guardian for Mrs. Edith Hill, to make care recommendations for Mrs. Hills care in the Fall of 2014.

I have heard the news that Mr. Eddie Harris is currently on life support and he is not expected to make it. I am very sorry to hear this sad news.

I would not recommend Mrs. Hill travel back from Florida to see Mr. Harris in his current state. I believe with her current level of memory impairment, state of capacity, and physical frailty it could be detrimental to her well-being.

Sincerely,

Kate H. Caldwell, MAG, CMC
Gerontologist/ Care Manager

ElderTree Care Management Services
WWW.ElderTreecare.com/ 703-424-   Office

Document 15
Eddie's Bank Account Statements

Visual evidence of multiple withdrawals made in a branch location. There were only two authorized individuals on the accounts, and one of them was on life support. A monthly check of $800 was issued to Eddie's nephew for rent. On December 24, 2014, a withdrawal of $9,400 was made from Eddie's account at a branch location.

Combined Statement of Accounts

Primary account number: ■ November 29, 2014 - December 24, 2014   ■ Page 1 of 5

EODC   016.

EDWARD C HARRISON
REBECCA MCDANIEL WRIGHT POA
                          AVE
ALEXANDRIA VA

Questions?
Available by phone 24 hours a day, 7 days a week:
1-800-TO-   (1-800-869-   )
TTY: 1-800-877-
En español: 1-877-727-
华语 1-800-288-   (6 am to 7 pm PT, M-F)

Online: .com
Write:
      P.O. Box
      Portland, OR

You and
Don't forget to notify us of your travel plans to help avoid issues when using your cards while traveling. It's easy to notify us of your travel plans online at .com/travelplan, through the mobile app, or by calling the phone number on the back of your card.

Account options
A check mark in the box indicates you have these convenient services with your account(s). Go to .com or call the number above if you have questions or if you would like to add new services.

Online Banking	☐	Direct Deposit	☑
Online Bill Pay	☐	Auto Transfer/Payment	☐
Online Statements	☐	Overdraft Protection	☑
Mobile Banking	☐	Debit Card	
My Spending Report	☐	Overdraft Service	☐

Summary of accounts

Checking/Prepaid and Savings

Account		Page	Account number	Ending balance last statement	Ending balance this statement
	Checking	2		9,156.38	299.51
	Savings	3		2,000.29	2,000.31
	Savings	4		54.29	55.29
		Total deposit accounts		$11,210.96	$2,355.11

LAW OFFICE

Primary account number: ■ November 29, 2014 - December 24, 2014 ■ Page 2 of 5

Checking

Activity summary

Beginning balance on 11/29	$9,156.38
Deposits/Additions	1,935.70
Withdrawals/Subtractions	- 10,792.57
Ending balance on 12/24	**$299.51**

Account number:
EDWARD C HARRISON
REBECCA MCDANIEL WRIGHT POA
Virginia account terms and conditions apply
For Direct Deposit use
Routing Number (RTN):

Overdraft Protection
Your account is linked to the following for Overdraft Protection:
■ Savings -

Transaction history

Date	Check Number	Description	Deposits/ Additions	Withdrawals/ Subtractions	Ending daily balance
12/1		Rrb Treas 310 Xxvr Ret 120114 Edward C Harrison	1,935.70		11,092.08
12/5	9093	Check		800.00	10,292.08
12/8	9094	Check		350.00	
12/8	^9095	Washgas Checkpaymt 141208 09095 3059251052		44.43	9,897.65
12/9	^9096	American Water Checkpymt 120814 09096 1027210037037467		25.32	9,872.33
12/10	^9097	AARP AARP 120914 09097 943432024470426		16.00	
12/10	9098	Check		8.38	9,847.95
12/15	^9099	Verizon Wireless Eckd511701 141211 09099 Bell, VA		116.44	
12/15		Dominion Vapower Elec Bill Dec 14 4104405002 Harrison,Edward.C		29.00	
12/15		Save As You Go Transfer Debit		1.00	9,701.51
12/24		Withdrawal Made In A Branch/Store		9,400.00	
12/24		Monthly Check Return/Image Stmt Fee		2.00	299.51
Ending balance on 12/24					**299.51**
Totals			**$1,935.70**	**$10,792.57**	

The Ending Daily Balance does not reflect any pending withdrawals or holds on deposited funds that may have been outstanding on your account when your transactions posted. If you had insufficient available funds when a transaction posted, fees may have been assessed.

^ Converted check: Check converted to an electronic format by your payee or designated representative. Checks converted to electronic format cannot be returned, copied or imaged.

Summary of checks written (checks listed are also displayed in the preceding Transaction history)

Number	Date	Amount	Number	Date	Amount	Number	Date	Amount
9093	12/5	800.00	9096	12/9	25.32	9098	12/10	8.38
9094	12/8	350.00	9097	12/10	16.00	9099	12/15	116.44
9095	12/8	44.43						

LAW OFFICE

Primary account number: ■ November 29, 2014 – December 24, 2014 ■ Page 3 of 5

Activity summary

Beginning balance on 11/29	$2,000.29
Deposits/Additions	0.02
Withdrawals/Subtractions	- 0.00
Ending balance on 12/24	$2,000.31

Account number:
EDWARD C HARRISON
REBECCA MCDANIEL WRIGHT POA
Virginia account terms and conditions apply
For Direct Deposit use
Routing Number (RTN):

Interest summary

Interest paid this statement	$0.02
Average collected balance	$2,000.29
Annual percentage yield earned	0.01%
Interest earned this statement period	$0.02
Interest paid this year	$0.20

Transaction history

Date	Description	Deposits/Additions	Withdrawals/Subtractions	Ending daily balance
12/24	Interest Payment	0.02		2,000.31
	Ending balance on 12/24			2,000.31
	Totals	$0.02	$0.00	

The Ending Daily Balance does not reflect any pending withdrawals or holds on deposited funds that may have been outstanding on your account when your transactions posted. If you had insufficient available funds when a transaction posted, fees may have been assessed.

Monthly service fee summary

For a complete list of fees and detailed account information, please see the Fee and Information Schedule and Account Agreement applicable to your account or talk to a banker. Go to .com/feefaq to find answers to common questions about the monthly service fee on your account.

Fee period 11/29/2014 - 12/24/2014		Standard monthly service fee $5.00	You paid $0.00
How to avoid the monthly service fee		Minimum required	This fee period
Have any ONE of the following account requirements			
· Minimum daily balance		$300.00	$2,000.29 ☑
· Daily automatic transfer from a	checking account	$1.00	$0.00 ☐ ^
· Save As You Go® transfer from a	checking account	$1.00	$0.00 ☐
· Monthly automatic transfer from a	checking account	$25.00	$0.00 ☐ ^
· The fee is waived when the primary account owner is under the age of 18 (19 in Alabama)			

^Zero is displayed because you did not meet the minimum amount required for a single transaction of this type.

LAW OFFICE

Account: November 29, 2014 - December 24, 2014 — Page 1 of 1

Online banking customers can view and print check images that have cleared since their last statement.

Check Images

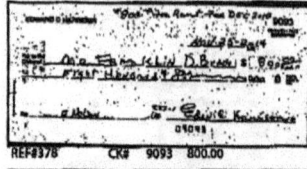

REF#8378 CK# 9093 800.00

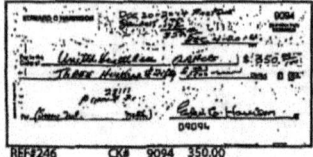

REF#246 CK# 9094 350.00

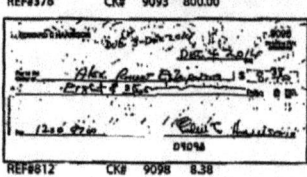

REF#8812 CK# 9098 8.38

LAW OFFICE   PAGE 06/09

Combined Statement of Accounts

Primary account number: ■ December 25, 2014 - January 28, 2015   ■ Page 1 of 5

EOOL   015

||||q||··|||·|||||||·|||||||·|·|||·||·|·|||·||·|·|||·||

EDWARD C HARRISON
REBECCA MCDANIEL WRIGHT POA
               AVE
ALEXANDRIA VA

Questions?

Available by phone 24 hours a day, 7 days a week:
1-800-TO-   (1-800-869-   )
TTY: 1-800-877-
En español: 1-877-727-
            1-800-288-   (6 am to 7 pm PT, M-F)

Online: .com
Write: Bank, N.A. (377)
         P.O. Box
         Portland, OR

You and

Thank you for being a loyal   customer. We value your trust in our company and look forward to continuing to serve you with your financial needs.

Account options

A check mark in the box indicates you have these convenient services with your account(s). Go to   .com or call the number above if you have questions or if you would like to add new services.

Online Banking	☐	Direct Deposit	☑
Online Bill Pay	☐	Auto Transfer/Payment	☐
Online Statements	☐	Overdraft Protection	☑
Mobile Banking	☐	Debit Card	☐
My Spending Report	☐	Overdraft Service	☐

Summary of accounts

Checking/Prepaid and Savings

Account		Page	Account number	Ending balance last statement	Ending balance this statement
	Checking	2		299.51	1,932.98
	Savings	2		2,000.31	0.00
	Savings	3		55.29	56.29
	Total deposit accounts			$2,355.11	$1,989.27

LAW OFFICE

Primary account number: ■ December 25, 2014 - January 28, 2015 ■ Page 3 of 5

Interest summary

Interest paid this statement	$0.00
Average collected balance	$117.21
Annual percentage yield earned	0.00%
Interest earned this statement period	$0.00
Interest paid this year	$0.00
Total Interest paid in 2014	$0.20

Transaction history

Date	Description		Deposits/ Additions	Withdrawals/ Subtractions	Ending daily balance
12/26	● Transfer to Harrison E Checking Ref #Ops	xxxxxx9923		1,700.00	300.31
1/2	Withdrawal Made in A Branch/Store			300.31	0.00
Ending balance on 1/28					0.00
Totals			$0.00	$2,000.31	

The Ending Daily Balance does not reflect any pending withdrawals or holds on deposited funds that may have been outstanding on your account when your transactions posted. If you had insufficient available funds when a transaction posted, fees may have been assessed.

● Indicates transactions that count toward Federal Reserve Board Regulation D limits. Please refer to your Account Agreement for complete details of the federally-mandated transaction limits for savings accounts.

Monthly service fee summary

For a complete list of fees and detailed account information, please see the Fee and Information Schedule and Account Agreement applicable to your account or talk to a banker. Go to .com/feefaq to find answers to common questions about the monthly service fee on your account.

Fee period 12/25/2014 - 01/28/2015	Standard monthly service fee $5.00	You paid $0.00

The bank has waived, or partially waived, the fee for this fee period. For the next fee period, you need to meet the requirement(s) to avoid the monthly service fee.

How to avoid the monthly service fee Have any ONE of the following account requirements		Minimum required	This fee period
・ Minimum daily balance		$300.00	$0.00 ☐
・ Daily automatic transfer from a	checking account	$1.00	$0.00 ☐ ^
・ Save As You Go® transfer from a	checking account	$1.00	$0.00 ☐
・ Monthly automatic transfer from a	checking account	$25.00	$0.00 ☐ ^
・ The fee is waived when the primary account owner is under the age of 18 (19 in Alabama)			

^Zero is displayed because you did not meet the minimum amount required for a single transaction of this type.

Savings

Activity summary

Beginning balance on 12/25	$55.29
Deposits/Additions	1.00
Withdrawals/Subtractions	- 0.00
Ending balance on 1/28	$56.29

Account number:
EDWARD C HARRISON
Virginia account terms and conditions apply
For Direct Deposit use
Routing Number (RTN):

Account: December 25, 2014 - January 28, 2015 — LAW OFFICE — Page 1 of 1

Online banking customers can view and print check images that have cleared since their last statement.

Check Images

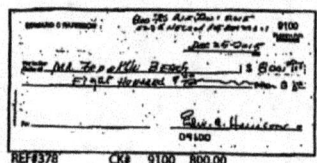

REF#378   CK# 9100   800.00

Document 16
Email

Rebecca's message notifying me that Eddie had passed away.

Mail - pebarber@　.com

Mail

Search Mail and People

⊕ New | ˅   ↶ Reply | ˅   🗑 Delete   🗄 Archive   Junk | ˅   Sweep   Move to ˅   •••   ↑ ↓

∧ Folders
 ˅ Inbox   996
   Junk Email   91
   Drafts   59
   Sent Items
   Deleted Items 225
   Archive
   Cary Cucinelli
  ∧ Cavalerej@
     newmail
   Conversation History
   Duplexes-Real Estε 1
   Jessica Niesen
   old stuff
   pictures
   rachel
   RSS Feeds
   Scheduled
   Spambox
   travel websites
   Unwanted

Eddie Harrison - passed away

R   rwrighttax@　.net
    Tue 12/30/2014, 6:35 PM
    You ˅

Patricia,

Eddie Harrison passed away today at Alexandria Inova Hospital.

Rebecca M. Wright
by Robert Wright

Document 17
Local MD Report

This letter shares the good news that my mother's health has improved following her return to my home in Florida.

Urgent Care
Suite
FL
Phone: (386)
Fax: (386)

Ramesh Patel, MD

January 19, 2015

Re: Edith Hill
   DOB 07/16/1918

To Whom It May Concern:

Since August 2012, Edith Hill has been under my care. She has resumed her medications and her medical condition has stabilized.

Edith has continued to gain weight since her recent visit of 12/08/2014. She is doing well. On January 5th, 2015 she had Medicare physical which revealed Mrs. Hill's emotional contentment. Should you have any questions, do not hesitate to contact me.

Sincerely,

Ramesh Patel, MD

Document 18
Seventh Report by guardian AD litem

The guardian ad litem, Joshua, officially recommends that my mother relocate to Florida with me. He also notes that the marriage was conducted in violation of the authority granted under the law.

VIRGINIA:
           IN THE CIRCUIT COURT OF THE CITY OF ALEXANDRIA

IN RE: EDITH HILL   ) Fiduciary No. CW11001379
    A person adjudicated incapacitated.   ) January 28, 2015 @ 10:00 a.m.

SEVENTH REPORT BY GUARDIAN AD LITEM

COMES NOW, Joshua E. Bushman, duly appointed Guardian *ad Litem* for EDITH HILL, and for his Seventh Report, but first response to the Rebecca Wright's Petition for Review of Decision of Guardian to Relocate Respondent to Florida and Sell Virginia Property, and the Guardian and Conservator's Petition to Authorize Ward's Relocation to Florida, hereby states the following:

1. Your Guardian ad Litem incorporates by reference all of his previously filed reports in this matter.

SUMMARY

2. Your Guardian ad Litem recommends the authority to transfer ward's relocation to Florida be granted. Your Guardian ad Litem believes that Mrs. Hill is currently located in a residence that is safe, receiving adequate medical care, and has previously lived for several months on a prior occasion.

INVESTIGATION

3. Your Guardian ad Litem has reviewed the pleadings filed by Rebecca Wright's counsel and by the Guardian and Conservator's counsel, spoken to the Guardian and Conservator, Patricia Barber, Curtis Hubbard, and Ernestine Yates:

    A.   Issue To Relocate Respondent To Florida:

The Guardian and Conservator believes the initial determination to send Ms. Hill to Florida was made as a temporary placement. It is reported that Rebecca Wright stopped administering, without consultation with the guardian, medication to Ms. Hill.

Since Ms. Hill's visit to Florida, she has resumed her medications, and her medical condition has stabilized. It was reported that she was underweight upon first leaving Rebecca Wright's care. From a social standpoint, Curtis Hubbard, her brother, reports the move has allowed him to speak with Ms. Hill almost daily. He states he was unable to reach his sister with any consistency while she remained in Virginia under Rebecca Wright's care, because Rebecca Wright would consistently have Ms. Hill moving from one place to the next. He reports that even when he made an appointment to see his sister, on the day of the appointment, just before leaving his house, Rebecca Wright called him and informed him they were going to a bar. Mr. Hubbard adjusted his plans accordingly to meet at the bar, so that he could be with his sister. At the bar, he reports the scene was inappropriate for an individual his age, let alone Edith's age. He reports they were seated right next to the speakers and that neither he, nor his sister, could hear one another. Furthermore, he reports that his sister appeared physically famished, and supported that contention, with an example: Mr. Hubbard described a moment that day where upon the table receiving some popcorn, Ms. Hill feverishly indulged herself as if she had not eaten the entire day. Mr. Hubbard believes that Rebecca negligently encouraged his sister to get up and dance. He feels the event was wholly inappropriate for someone Edith's age. In addition, he believes that Rebecca Wright's comments to the media are untrue and has embarrassed the family in an effort to exploit his sister. He is in favor of Mrs. Hill remaining in Florida, and for this cause to be transferred to that jurisdiction.

Your Guardian ad Litem spoke with Ernestine Yates. Ms. Yates is easily agitated by the factual underpinnings in which Ms. Wright has brought this case, as well as the previous motion to have her removed in late 2013. She believes that this court hearing is another attempt for Rebecca Wright to exploit her mother. She is emphatic in her support for her mother to reside in Florida, and supports that this cause be transferred there.

B. Sale of the Real Property in Virginia:

This issue has been litigated and the only change that has occurred is that Ms. Hill's needs are continually not met while she resides in the Alexandria property. The Court Order dated February 24, 2014 while the parties were at the courthouse was handwritten by your Guardian ad Litem with Patricia Barber, Rebecca Wright, and their respective counselors. It is your Guardian ad Litem's understanding that Rebecca Wright was to pay for the repairs and that the repairs were to be determined by a geriatric care manager or a neutral third party. She failed to do so then. The house is inappropriate for the respondent's medical needs: the bedrooms are upstairs, in order to get upstairs a narrow staircase must be traversed. There is no assistive equipment installed, and it has been reported the narrowness of the stairwell would not support the appropriate equipment. This is one example of the residence being unfit to support the needs of the respondent. Since the house is unfit for Mrs. Hill to reside and if she must reside outside of the home based on her needs, the Medicaid program will not allow her to maintain ownership of the residence, except in limited circumstances. The listing of the residence for sale is a necessity under the Federal Medicaid regulations as administered by the Commonwealth of Virginia, Department Medical Assistance Services.

RECOMMENDATIONS

4. Your Guardian ad Litem believes there is no order that this Court can deliver which will be agreeable to all three daughters. Each and every time this case is before the Court, the most amenable agreement that has ever been reached is for two out of three daughters to agree. This situation does not differ. Initially, this court granted Ms. Yates as guardian and conservator, and during Ms. Yates tenure, Mrs. Hill relocated to Ms. Yates' residence after the death of Ms. Hill's only son. Ms. Hill split her time between Maryland and Florida, while predominantly residing in Maryland. Ms. Wright and Patricia Barber then agreed to a split arrangement between them in a greater effort to remove Ms. Yates as guardian and conservator. Upon that Court Order, Ms. Hill has stayed predominantly in Virginia under Ms. Wright's care. During that period of guardianship, Ms. Wright without authorization or notice to the co-guardian, had her mother married contrary to the powers authorized under the law; moreover, the marriage was done without notifying either of the other daughters. This Court appointed the current guardian and conservator, a non-family member. Mrs. Hill had remained in Virginia under essentially the care of Ms. Wright since the last court decision. During that tenure, it is reported that Ms. Hill's health has been subject to an unreasonable withdraw of medication. Your Guardian ad litem recommends this court authorize the relocation of the Edith Hill to Florida as her health is reported have stabilized.

WHEREFORE, having answered the Petition previously exhibited against EDITH HILL, your Guardian ad Litem submits her interests to the Court and asks that no Decree be entered to her prejudice.

Joshua E. Bushman
Guardian Ad Litem for
EDITH HILL

VSB number 74729
Road, suite
Arlington, Virginia
(703) 845-
(703) 845- Facsimile
Josh.Bushman@ .com

Certificate of Service

I do hereby certify that a true and accurate copy of the foregoing Report by Guardian Ad Litem was transmitted via facsimile and/or mailed, first class mail, postage prepaid, this 26 day of January, 2015, to:

Kenneth E. Labowitz
Labowitz Dingman P.C.
Street, Suite
Alexandria, Virginia

Ernestine Yates

Benjamin G. Chew, Esq
Rory Adams, Esq.
Manatt, Phelps & Phillips LLP
street NW, Suite
Washington D.C.,

Patricia Barber

Curtis Hubbard

Joshua E. Bushman.
Guardian ad Litem for
EDITH HILL

Document 19
Care Assessment

This care assessment report was conducted at my residence in Florida. The care manager provided her strongest recommendation for me to care for my mother. The report also refutes the allegations of abuse made against my husband, Rayfield.

CARE ASSESSMENT
Date: February 10th 2015
Client: Mrs. Edith Hill
Completed by: Kate Caldwell, MA, CMC

Overview

Mrs. Edith Hill is a 96-year-old woman who currently resides with her daughter Mrs. Patricia Barber at   Place,   Florida. I last assessed Mrs. Hill on October 17th 2014, at   St. Alexandria, Virginia, when she resided with her daughter Ms. Rebecca Wright. My first assessment of Mrs. Hill was December 17th 2013, when she resided at   Lane, Baltimore, Maryland, with Ms. Ernestine Yates, her eldest daughter. I have been requested to complete a comprehensive assessment of Mrs. Hill's care needs by Mr. Kenneth Labowitz, Attorney at Law, who represents the Guardian, Ms. Jessica Niesen, Attorney at Law. This assessment will include her current level of care needs and recommendations on the appropriate living environment.

On February 10th 2015, I met for three hours with Mrs. Hill at Mrs. Patricia Barber's home in   Florida. Upon arrival I found Mrs. Hill sitting in the kitchen eating her breakfast. Mrs. Barber and her husband Mr. Rayfield Barber were also present. The following report details the information from this February 10th meeting.

Mrs. Hill had just finished a full breakfast and was drinking a glass of water when I arrived. She looked well groomed and was wearing a purple sweat suit. She was relaxed and responsive to my questions: she told stories I had heard in the past about being a bus driver and singing in the church choir. She seemed more focused and better able to respond to the questions I was asking her than during my last visit.

I observed Mrs. Hill ambulating with her cane from the kitchen to the living room couch with stand-by assistance. Mrs. Barber stated that the appropriate walker had been ordered by the physical therapist. Mrs. Hill requires stand-by assistance transferring to and from a seated position.

Mrs. Barber has a back up certified caregiver arranged with Granny Nannies as well as a housekeeper when needed. Mrs. Barber clearly understands the commitment in being the full-time caregiver for her mother. Mr. Barber supports his wife in caring for Mrs. Hill, although he travels for work on average 50% of the time.

ElderTree Care Management Services
www.ElderTreecare.com/ 703-424-   Office

Recent Medical Appointments

Mrs. Barber shared with me Mrs. Hill's current medical status along with reports from her physicians. On December 16th 2014 soon after her arrival in Florida Mrs. Hill attended an appointment with Dr. Ndum of Florida Cancer Specialists in reference to Mrs. Hill's 2011 diagnosis of breast cancer. The following are notes from Dr. Ndum: Much improvement overall on current medication. Weight loss of 6 lbs. in eight months is noted. Not a candidate for surgery or radiation therapy. Was off Letrozole for a while when living with other daughter up north, currently stable. Continue with current management.

Mrs. Hill's current primary care physician is Dr. Ramesh Patel. Mrs. Hill had a complete Medicare physical on January 5th 2015 in which the doctor noted her emotional contentment. He stated that she had resumed her prescribed medication and that her medical condition had stabilized. Dr. Patel wrote a prescription for physical therapy in the home for strength training and fall prevention. Confident Care of Florida, a licensed and accredited home health agency that provides skilled medical care in the home, was contacted. Mrs. Hill now receives physical therapy three times per week, which is covered by Medicare. According to Mrs. Barber the physical therapist is well suited for Mrs. Hill and Mrs. Hill enjoys the sessions.

On January 5th 2015, Mrs. Hill attended an appointment with Dr. Makowski, an ophthalmologist to review the status of Mrs. Hill's glaucoma. He recommended that Mrs. Hill continue taking Travatan Z drops in both eyes at nighttime. This is the first time I was aware of the glaucoma and the treatment plan.

Medical/Health

Diagnoses:
Bilateral Breast Cancer
Dementia (cause unknown)
Hypertension
Osteopenia
Degenerative Arthritis
Glaucoma
Bilateral Cataract Surgery

ElderTree Care Management Services
www.ElderTreecare.com/ 703-424-   Office

Current Medication list:

Medication	Dose	Reason	Physician
Namenda	10 MG	Dementia	Dr. Ndum
Letrozole	2.5MG	Breast Cancer	Dr. Ndum
Losartan HCTZ	100/25 MG	Hypertension	Dr. Ndum
Travatan Z drops	0.004%	Glaucoma	Dr. Makowski

Current Physicians

Dr. Ramesh Patel Primary Care Physician	Drive Suite FL	Phone: (386) Fax: (386)
Dr. Philip Ndum Oncologist	Medical Parkway Suite FL	Phone: (386) Fax: (855)
Dr. Michael Makowski Ophthalmologist	Drive Suite FL	Phone: (386) Fax: (386)

Current Living Environment:

The Barber family home is situated on a cul-de-sac in a golf community. The one-level ranch-style home was clean, organized, and nicely decorated. Traditional to a Florida style home there are sliding glass doors and windows that open up to the interior courtyard, creating an indoor/outdoor living space. Mrs. Hills private bedroom was nicely appointed, there was a couch where Mrs. Barber often sleeps in the case that her mother needs assistance in the night. There was a portable commode next to the bed for nighttime use. Next to the bed-room was a bathroom with a built-in shower bench and a hand-held showerhead, which Mrs. Barber uses when she assists her mother showering two or three times a week. Mrs. Barber stated that she would like to install a shower bar to give her mother something to hold onto as she steps into the shower. There are two other bedrooms in the home. One is for Mrs. Barber and her husband and the other is for their grandson Patrick. Patrick is in the third grade and was in school during my visit. Please see appendix (A) for photos of the home.

Nutrition/Hydration:

Mrs. Hill currently weighs 102 pounds; this is up from 98 when she first arrived in Florida. Mrs. Barber reports that her mother has a good appetite and that she especially enjoys vanilla cake for dessert after dinner. Mrs. Hill was wearing her dentures. Mrs.

ElderTree Care Management Services
www.ElderTreecare.com/ 703-424-   Office

great-grandson and watching him play. Mrs. Hill also enjoys going out to get her hair done.

Throughout my visit I asked Mrs. Hill how she was feeling physically and emotionally, using questions from the Geriatric Depression Scale: (How are your spirits? Are you in good spirits most of the time?) She answered my questions appropriately and positively. When I asked her about Eddie, she responded, "Who?" While pointing to Mrs. Barber I asked, "Does Patricia take good care of you?" She said, "Oh yes, she cares for me like I cared for my mother" and went on to explain. I asked her this same question later privately and she responded the same way while smiling and laughing. I asked how she felt about living with her great-grandson Patrick and she talked about how busy he is and how much she enjoys watching him. I asked Mrs. Hill how she felt about Rayfield and she said "Oh, Pat's husband. Oh yes, he is very nice."

During my visit I administered the Short Portable Mental Status Questionnaire in place of or the full Mini Mental Status Exam. Mrs. Hill was very willing to answer my questions, although she was only able to answer two questions and scored at the Moderate Intellectual Function level.

Summary and Recommendations:

Mrs. Hill lives with her daughter, Mrs. Patricia Barber, who is her primary caregiver. Mrs. Barber has support systems in place for respite care when needed. In the short time Mrs. Barber has had Mrs. Hill living with her she has taken all of the necessary steps to care for her mother and to create the highest quality of life possible for Mrs. Hill. Mrs. Barber is providing a loving, safe, and predictable environment for her mother.

I have had the opportunity to assess Mrs. Hill under the care of Ms. Ernestine Yates, Ms. Rebecca Wright, and Mrs. Patricia Barber. It is my highest recommendation that Mrs. Hill be allowed the peace and dignity that Mrs. Barber has clearly demonstrated she can provide for her mother. If at any time Mrs. Hill's care needs should exceed what Mrs. Barber feels she can provide, Mrs. Barber should consider moving Mrs. Hill to a community that can adequately meet her overall care needs.

Report prepared and submitted by:

Kate H. Caldwell, MA, CMC
ElderTree Care Management

ElderTree Care Management Services
www.ElderTreecare.com/ 703-424-   Office

Document 20
Jessica niesen's response to rebecca wright's first set of interrogatories

Successor guardian and conservator Jessica Niesen responded to question 8, stating that she received an email from Rebecca on the night of Eddie's death informing her that his remains were in the morgue.

VIRGINIA:

IN THE CIRCUIT COURT OF THE CITY OF ALEXANDRIA

IN RE: APPOINTMENT OF A)
GUARDIAN AND CONSERVATOR) Fiduciary No. CW11001379
FOR EDITH HILL)

JESSICA NIESEN'S RESPONSE TO REBECCA WRIGHT'S FIRST SET OF INTERROGATORIES

COMES NOW Jessica Niesen as Successor Guardian and Successor Conservator for Edith Hill, a person deemed under a disability, by counsel, with her Answers to Rebecca Wright's First Set of Interrogatories.

Interrogatories

1. Please identify by name and address witnesses proposed to be introduced at the March 2, 2015 *ore tenus* hearing and for each such witness please summarize what personal knowledge that person has of the facts alleged in, or reasonably implied from, the pleadings in this matter, including, but not limited to, Ms. Wright's January 14, 2015 Petition and Ms. Niesen's January 21, 2015 Petition.

Answer:

Ms. Niesen objects to this Interrogatory as not reasonably calculated to lead to the discovery of admissible evidence. By its terms, the Interrogatory is seeking the identities of those intended to be called as witnesses and is not intended to seek information within the scope of permissible discovery.

The parties have agreed to exchange their lists of witnesses in advance of the hearing set for March 2, 2015 and their marked exhibits.

Notwithstanding such objection and without waiving same, Ms. Niesen intends to testify concerning her actions and decisions as Successor Guardian and Successor Conservator. She will testify from her experience in dealing with Edith Hill since the time of her appointment and qualification as Successor Guardian and Successor Conservator, as well as her dealings with Rebecca Wright and Patricia Barber and others in the context of her role for Ms. Hill.

Kate Caldwell is also expected to testify regarding her assessments of Ms. Hill in December 2013, October 2014 and February 2015, including Ms. Caldwell's personal observations of Ms. Hill in the settings of the home at _____ Street, Alexandria, Virginia in 2014, and in the home of Mrs. Barber in _____ Florida, in 2015. Ms. Caldwell is expected to testify concerning her interactions with Ms. Wright in the 2014 assessment and with Mrs. Barber in the 2015 assessment. She is expected to testify further regarding the physical conditions in each setting and the relationship of those conditions to Ms. Hill's personal and medical needs and the availability of alternative living arrangements.

Ms. Niesen has not yet determined who else she may call as a witness, but will provide her witness list in advance of the hearing date. She will also reserve the right to call any witness identified on behalf of Ms. Wright or the Guardian *ad Litem*.

2. In accordance with Rule 4:1(b)(4)(a)(i) of the Rules of the Supreme Court of Virginia, please identify all persons whom you expect to call as an expert witness at the March 2, 2015 *ore tenus* hearing. For each person identified, please state the subject matter on which the expert is expected to testify, including but not limited to, the substance of the facts and opinions to which the expert is expected to testify and a summary of the grounds for each opinion.

Answer:

Ms. Niesen intends to call Kate Caldwell, a professional care manager, to testify concerning her personal observations of Ms. Hill; Ms. Hill's medical condition; Ms. Hill's need for specific care in light of those medical conditions; the nature of the conditions in the residence located at   Street, Alexandria, Virginia   , and in the home of Patricia Barber in   Florida, where Ms. Hill presently resides in terms of Ms. Hill's needs, capabilities, and comfort; the nature of the social interactions available to Ms. Hill in each location; the interactions between Ms. Hill on the one hand and Rebecca Wright and Mrs. Barber on the other hand in terms of the needs and care of Ms. Hill in each locale; the history and availability of consistent and appropriate medical care for Ms. Hill; and the value and availability of alternative living and care arrangements for Ms. Hill, other than having care provided in homes occupied by Ms. Wright in Alexandria and Mrs. Barber in Florida.

Copies of Ms. Caldwell's reports of her assessments made in December 2013, October 2014, and February 2015 are attached as "Exhibit A."

Ms. Caldwell will testify as to her findings within her capacity as a professional geriatric care manager. A copy of her resume is attached as "Exhibit B."

Ms. Caldwell's opinions and findings are set forth in the assessment reports as provided.

3. Please describe in detail, including estimated costs, the renovations or repairs you believe are reasonably required to make the residence at   Street suitable for Ms. Hill to reside there.

Answer:

According the geriatric care manager's assessment, it is not safe or appropriate for a woman of Edith's age and mobility to be forced to navigate the steep flight of stairs on a daily basis to access her sleeping space and the only bathroom on site. The only solution would be to build out a small room and bathroom to the property on the main floor.

Without bringing various home repair experts on site, Ms. Niesen cannot give any more than a guess as to an estimate to repair or renovate the Property to an appropriate condition suitable for Ms. Hill. Ms. Niesen has been unable to get a formal appraisal because Ms. Wright has refused all previous requests to provide keys to the residence and Ms. Niesen therefore has no access for these contractors. Ms. Niesen made a rough estimate previously of $25,000.00, but that does not include a new bedroom and bathroom on the first floor. There is possibly more expense if there needs to be a rezoning or there are other land use issues with adding new rooms to the building.

4. Please describe in detail, including estimated costs, the medically necessary care, such as a home healthcare worker, you believe is reasonably required to enable Ms. Hill to reside at   Street.

Answer:

Counsel and Ms. Wright were previously provided with copy of the geriatric care manager's assessment and report from October 2014, attached in "Exhibit A." As the report indicates Ms. Hill is considered to be a "one-on-one assist" for all ADLs. She therefore requires 24/7 onsite assistance.

Aides may be retained from numerous local certified companies at approximately $20.00 per hour, depending on the aide, their level of training, and the company supplying the aides. This would result in approximately $15,000.00 a month in care charges. This does not include any nursing level care or the oversight by a geriatric care manager, both of which would be billed at a higher rate.

A less expensive option would be a live-in aid through one of these professional companies. The cheapest rates Ms. Niesen has been able to locate are $200.00 per day. This option requires that the aide have a bedroom to sleep in, which the   Street home does not currently have with Ms. Wright staying in the bedroom and without the extra bedroom for Ms. Hill on the first floor.

5. Please describe in detail, including estimated costs, the reasonable expenses for ongoing upkeep of the   Street property necessary to enable Ms. Hill to live there.

Answer:

The home requires typical upkeep: yard maintenance, filters and yearly checks on heating and AC systems, utilities, and insurance. This could be as little as a few of hundred dollars a month. The status of more expensive repair items such as the roof is unknown.

Taxes are covered by the City low income seniors program. This does not consider medical care or food or any miscellaneous expenses such as clothing, transportation or entertainment.

6. Describe Ms. Hill's current medical status including, but not limited to, a description of current medical conditions, acute or chronic, and whether Ms. Hill is continent and

ambulatory. To the extent you have personal knowledge sufficient to respond to this Interrogatory, please describe the basis of your personal knowledge.

Answer:

The geriatric care manager's reports best speak to Ms. Hill's ongoing medical conditions and needs. Attached and marked as "Exhibit C" are letters from physicians who are currently treating Ms. Hill in Florida. These are all doctors who have previously treated Ms. Hill when she was residing in Florida with Mrs. Barber from approximately July 2012 through January 2013, and again from approximately March 2014 through April 2014.

Ms. Hill's weight on arrival in Florida in December 2014 was down to 98 pounds. Within approximately 10 days in Florida and receiving proper meals and rest, Ms. Hill regained four pounds of the approximate 15 she had lost in the three and one-half months during which Ms. Wright was caring for her.

Ms. Hill is currently continent, for the most part. She has occasional accidents and, given how slowly she moves, it is sometimes difficult to get her to the bathroom on time. As indicated in the care manager's October report, she is ambulatory with the heavy use of her cane and one-on-one assistance for transport. She is going to be 97 this coming summer, and her condition is normal for her age. She will only continue to require more assistance.

Ms. Hill continues to have dementia, high blood pressure, glaucoma and cancer along with all simple age-related frailties.

7. Describe by date, duration and purpose all in-person visits Ms. Hill has had from family members, friends, you, and the guardian ad litem since December 6, 2014.

Answer:

Ms. Hill is visited by Patricia Barber every day, as she has been living with her. She is also visited by other family members who live in Patricia Barber's house. Ms. Niesen has not visited Mrs. Barber in Florida, nor has Joshua Bushman, the Guardian *ad Litem*.

8. Describe the current location and disposition of Eddie Harrison's physical remains.

Answer:

Ms. Niesen received an email from Ms. Wright the night that Mr. Harrison had died, stating that his remains were in the morgue. With the help of Ms. Yates and Mrs. Barber, Ms. Niesen contacted Mr. Harrison's nephew. He provided Ms. Niesen with the name of the cemetery where Mr. Harrison's second wife was buried and where he had purchased a plot for himself.

Ms. Niesen made arrangements to have Mr. Harrison's body cremated and will retain possession of the cremains until it can be determined if he should be buried next to his second wife in the plot that he chose and purchased for himself or if one of Edith's family members would like to keep the ashes and eventually place the couple together after Edith's passing.

Due to the fact that Mr. Harrison's financial accounts were emptied by parties unknown in the amount of $9,400 on December 24, 2014, after his admission to the hospital, Ms. Niesen paid these expenses from Ms. Hill's limited finances.

9. Describe the layout of Patricia Barber's residence, including the number of floors, bedrooms, and bathrooms.

Answer:

Mrs. Barber's residence is one-story, and it has three bedrooms and three bathrooms (one bathroom has an entrance only from the outside, as is typical with some Florida homes).

10. Identify by name, age, and relation, the people currently living in Patricia Barber's residence.

Answer:

Patricia Barber, daughter, age 68. Rayfield Barber, son-in-law, age 69, lives in Chicago, Illinois. He is due to retire soon and will move into Mrs. Barber's residence when he retires. Patrick (as he is a minor Ms. Niesen withholds his last name), great-grandson, age 8.

11. To the extent you believe that the _____ Street home cannot be an appropriate living environment for Ms. Hill, please state all material facts supporting this belief.

Answer:

As set out in her responses to 4. and 5., above, the care of Ms. Hill at _____ Street requires both the engagement of aides and significant renovation of the premises. The expense of those elements of Ms. Hill's care are in addition to the ongoing debt that Ms. Hill has incurred, including the unpaid fees to the Guardian *ad Litem* and the expense of Ms. Niesen's counsel in the current proceeding.

Ms. Niesen considers the _____ Street home in the context that Rebecca Wright will inevitably be involved with her mother's residence there. Past experience with Ms. Wright has convinced Ms. Niesen that Ms. Wright and her judgment are incompatible with the best interests of Ms. Hill. Ms. Wright is incapable of working collaboratively with Ms. Niesen toward a common approach to Ms. Hill, her medical and personal needs, and the use of Ms. Hill's resources.

Ms. Hill has materially benefitted from the time that she has spent most recently in Florida. She has received consistent medical care, including administration of medications as prescribed. She is permitted to live in a calm environment with appropriate socialization and stimuli, as opposed to the conditions under which she was living when she most recently resided in Alexandria with Ms. Wright. Ms. Hill's funds are accounted for, again in distinction from her experience with Ms. Wright. Ms. Hill is gaining weight, as opposed to the weight loss she suffered while residing with Ms. Hill. The weather in the winter is more comfortable for Ms. Hill in Florida.

The totality of the circumstances in comparing the two locations leads Ms. Niesen to the conclusion that, in the exercise of her judgment as the appointed Successor Guardian and Successor Conservator for Ms. Hill, the appropriate application of Ms. Niesen's discretion is for Ms. Hill to reside with Mrs. Barber in Florida. If and when funds become available from the sale of the   Street property, Ms. Niesen will consider the possibility of moving Ms. Hill to an appropriate care facility in the vicinity of Mrs. Barber's residence, if she determines that such a move will be in her judgment the best application of her discretion as Successor Guardian and Successor Conservator.

_____
Jessica Niesen, Successor Guardian and
Successor Conservator for Edith Hill

City/County of Arlington
Commonwealth of Virginia

Subscribed and sworn to before me by Jessica Niesen, Successor Guardian and Successor Conservator for Edith Hill, this _20th_ day of _February_, 2015.

_____
Notary Public
My commission expires: August 31, 2018
SEAL:

ALLISON MURPHY
NOTARY PUBLIC
REG. # 7623303
COMMONWEALTH OF VIRGINIA
MY COMMISSION EXPIRES AUGUST 31, 2018

_____
Kenneth E. Labowitz - Virginia Bar No. 16580
kel@   .com
Anne M. Heishman - Virginia Bar No. 65540
amh@   .com
Jacqueline T. Sandler – Virginia Bar No. 87977
jts@   .com
Dingman Labowitz P.C.
          Street, Suite
Alexandria, Virginia
Telephone: 703.519
Facsimile: 703.519
Counsel for Jessica Niesen,
Successor Guardian and Successor Conservator for Edith Hill

CERTIFICATE OF SERVICE

I hereby certify that a copy of the foregoing discovery response has been served by United States Mail, first class postage prepaid, and emailed, if available upon the following persons, this 24 day of February, 2015:

Benjamin Chew
Manatt, Phelps & Phillips, LLP
      Street NW, Suite
Washington, DC
bchew@   .com
Counsel for Rebecca Wright

Joshua Bushman, Esq.
Bushman Law Group
              Road, Suite
Arlington, VA
josh.bushman@   .com
Guardian ad Litem for Edith Hill

Patricia Barber

           FL
pebarber@   .com

Ernestine Yates
           Lane
Baltimore, MD

Curtis Hubbard
           Drive
Silver Spring, MD

_____
Kenneth E. Labowitz

Document 21
Order

Page four outlines the amounts owed to various individuals, which resulted in a lien against Mom's real property that was required to be settled within six months of her passing. Exhibit C in this document outlines the estimated average annual cost of a CNA in 2015.

VIRGINIA:

IN THE CIRCUIT COURT OF THE CITY OF ALEXANDRIA

In re: Estate of Edith Hill)
) Fiduciary No. CW11001379
)

ORDER

CAME ON for hearing the Petition filed on behalf of Rebecca Wright for Review of the Decision of the Guardian and Conservator for Respondent Edith Hill to Relocate Ms. Hill to Florida and to Sell Ms. Hill's Virginia Property and the Opposition thereto filed on behalf of Jessica Niesen as Guardian and Conservator to Relocate Ms. Hill's Residence to Florida. Upon consideration of the evidence presented on behalf of Ms. Wright, the Guardian and Conservator, and the Guardian *ad litem* for Ms. Hill and the argument of counsel, it is hereby

ORDERED:

1. Ms. Hill is to remain in Florida at the home of Patricia Barber until such time as the renovation of Ms. Hill's residence located at   Street in Alexandria is completed and approved by Kate Caldwell and Jessica Niesen as safe, habitable, and appropriate for Ms. Hill and the care that she requires. Such agreement and approval shall not be unreasonably withheld.

2. Ms. Caldwell and Ms. Niesen shall promptly secure a proposal from a licensed contractor with an estimate of the costs for necessary renovations of the   Street property as set forth above.

3. Ms. Caldwell and Ms. Niesen shall also provide an estimate of the costs for home care for Ms. Hill in her residence on Princess Street for the period of one year from the

resumption of her residence there as deemed appropriate for her needs, as well as an estimate for Ms. Caldwell's fees for management of Ms. Hill's care on an annual basis.

4. The estimates for the renovation work for the _____ Street residence and for the provision of home care and care management for Ms. Hill in that residence shall be provided to counsel for Ms. Wright with the understanding that counsel will transmit such estimates to Cher (the "Benefactor"). Counsel for Ms. Wright shall promptly advise Ms. Caldwell and Ms. Niesen of acceptance or rejection of the estimates.

5. As a condition of the return of Ms. Hill to reside in the _____ Street residence and promptly upon the acceptance of the estimates provided to counsel for Ms. Wright, the Benefactor shall pay into the trust account maintained by Ms. Niesen sufficient funds to cover the anticipated costs for the renovation of the premises and a full year's expense for the care costs, including direct care and care management provided by Ms. Caldwell and her firm, Elder Tree Care Management Services.

Prior to the deposit into her trust account of such funds from the Benefactor, Ms. Niesen shall enter into a secured conservator bond in an appropriate amount.

Within 30 days of the anniversary each year of Ms. Hill's return to her residence in the _____ Street property, the Benefactor shall pay into the trust account maintained by Ms. Niesen sufficient funds to cover an additional year of care and care management for Ms. Hill in her residence. Any funds remaining provided by the Benefactor at Ms. Hill's death or permanent relocation from her residence shall be returned to the Benefactor.

6. The Court intends for the professional services provided to the date of entry of this Order by the care manager, the Guardian and Conservator, her counsel in this proceeding, and the Guardian *ad litem* to be paid from Ms. Hill's assets. The sole source of funds with which

2

to pay for such services is the equity in Ms. Hill's residence on ____ Street. The Court finds that there is sufficient equity in the property to compensate for the professional services provided to date.

The Guardian and Conservator is hereby authorized to enter into a loan transaction secured by the equity in Ms. Hill's ____ Street property in sufficient amount to pay the total compensation awarded herein. Ms. Niesen is specifically authorized to execute the documents necessary to enter into the loan transaction and to impose a lien against Ms. Hill's property for the repayment of the loan at the time of the sale of the property.

The authority previously granted to Ms. Niesen to list the property for sale remains in effect, subject to the requirement for the Court's approval of any proposed contract of sale, but limited to the circumstances of either default of the terms of this Order or Ms. Hill's permanent relocation to a residence other than her ____ Street home. Ms. Niesen is directed to seek court approval for a permanent relocation of Ms. Hill other than to the ____ Street residence.

Specifically, if the Benefactor fails to accept the estimates for the costs of renovation and care and care management or fails to promptly deliver the funds set out in this Order to Ms. Niesen, then default has occurred in the terms of this Order and Ms. Niesen is authorized to proceed to list the ____ Street property for sale, subject to the stated requirement.

7. Ms. Caldwell shall approve in advance any visitation with Ms. Hill by family members wherever she is located, and visitation shall be under such circumstances and conditions as she directs.

8. Ms. Niesen is to take all appropriate steps to insure to the extent possible telephone access with Ms. Hill.

9. No party to this proceeding shall engage in, permit, or cause Ms. Hill to be ~~filed~~ filmed, recorded, or interviewed by outside parties, absent further order of this Court.

10. To the extent that the provisions of this Order have not addressed the relief sought by Ms. Wright in her Petition to Review Decision of Guardian to Relocate Respondent to Florida and Sell Virginia Property and the Guardian and Conservator's Petition to Authorize Respondent's Relocation to Florida, those matters are DENIED.

11. The following compensation is awarded for services to Ms. Hill through the date of entry of this Order, with the funds to pay such compensation to be obtained through the loan transaction anticipated as set forth in ¶ 6, above. To the extent that such compensation has not been paid at the time of Ms. Hill's death, the awards set out herein shall constitute liens against the title to the property located at   Street, Alexandria, Virginia and constitute claims against the Estate of Ms. Hill.

Kate Caldwell is awarded the sum of $ 2,228.75 ;

Jessica Niesen is awarded the sum of $ 13,200 ;

Joshua Bushman is awarded the sum of $ 22,714.09 ; (this amount represents Mr. Bushman's compensation for his work on Ms. Hill's behalf) JCC

Kenneth Labowitz and the firm of Dingman Labowitz P.C. is awarded the sum of $ 28,900 .

The Clerk is directed to spread this Order among the land records maintained for the City of Alexandria.

IT IS SO ORDERED.

ENTERED this __27__ day of __March__ 2015.

_____
The Honorable James C. Clark

SEEN AND AGREED:

_____
Benjamin G. Chew (VSB No. 29113)
Nigel L. Wilkinson (VSB No. 46500)
Rory E. Adams (VSB No. 76452)
MANATT, PHELPS & PHILLIPS LLP
　　　　　　　　Avenue NW, Suite
Washington, DC

Counsel for Rebecca Wright

SEEN AND *Agreed*   :
/s/ Kenneth E. Labowitz
Kenneth Labowitz, Esq. (VSB No. 16580)
Anne Heishman, Esq. (VSB No. 65840)
Jacqueline Sandler, Esq. (VSB No. 87977)
DINGMAN LABOWITZ P.C.
　　　Street, Suite
Alexandria, VA

Counsel to Guardian and Conservator Jessica J. Niesen, Esq.

SEEN AND *Agreed*   :
/s/ Joshua E. Bushman
Joshua Bushman, Esq. (VSB No. 74729)
BUSHMAN LAW GROUP
　　　　　Road, Suite
Arlington, VA

Guardian ad Litem for Edith Hill

203063757.1

CLOSING - EXCERPT 3/2/2015

Page 1

1 VIRGINIA:
2 IN THE CIRCUIT COURT OF THE CITY OF ALEXANDRIA
3
4 ----------------------
5 IN RE: EDITH HILL   Fiduciary No.
6 A person adjudicated incapacitated CWI1001579
7 ----------------------
8   Alexandria, Virginia
9   March 2, 2015
10
11
12
13   EXCERPT OF THE CLOSING ARGUMENTS
14
15
16
17   The excerpt of the above-entitled matter
18 came on to be heard before the HONORABLE JAMES C.
19 CLARK, Judge in and for the Circuit Court of the
20 City of Alexandria located at   Street,
21 Alexandria, Virginia, commencing at 3:53 p.m., when
22 were present on behalf of the respective parties.

Page 2

1   APPEARANCES
2
3 ON BEHALF OF REBECCA WRIGHT:
4   BENJAMIN B. CHEW, ESQUIRE
5   NIGEL L. WILKINSON, ESQUIRE
6   RORY E. ADAMS, ESQUIRE
7   Manatt, Phelps & Phillips, LLP
8   Street, Northwest, Suite
9   Washington, D.C.
10   (202) 585-
11   (202) 585-   - fax
12
13 ON BEHALF OF JESSICA J. NIESEN:
14   KENNETH E. LABOWITZ, ESQUIRE
15   JACQUELINE T. SANDLER, ESQUIRE
16   Labowitz Dingman, P.C.
17   Street
18   Suite
19   Alexandria, Virginia
20   (703) 519-
21   (703) 519-   - fax
22 (Appearances continued on the next page.)

Page 3

1 APPEARANCES (continued):
2
3 GUARDIAN AD LITEM:
4   JOSHUA E. BUSHMAN, ESQUIRE
5   Bushman Law Group
6   Road
7   Suite
8   Arlington, Virginia
9   (703) 845-
10   (703) 845-   - fax
11
12 GUARDIAN:
13   JESSICA J. NIESEN, ESQUIRE
14   Jessica J. Niesen, Attorney at Law
15   North   Street
16   Suite
17   Arlington, Virginia
18   (703) 527-
19   (703) 527-   - fax
20
21
22

Page 4

1   PROCEEDINGS
2 --------------
3 (The court reporter was previously sworn.)
4 (Whereupon, at 3:53 p.m., the excerpt of
5 the closing arguments commenced.)
6   MR. CHEW: Your Honor, I would like to do a
7 short closing and then propose something that I
8 think -- I hope should be reasonable, serve the best
9 interest of Edith Hill, and make everybody
10 reasonably happy.
11   THE COURT: Mr. Chew, if you can come up
12 with that, I'll be all ears.
13   MR. CHEW: I'm going to do my best -- very
14 quickly because I know the Court has listened very
15 carefully all day.
16   THE COURT: No, you take all the time you
17 need because it -- I mean, you know, I mean, we try
18 and -- we try and lighten the mood a little bit,
19 but, you know, she deserves the best we can give her
20 and you all have worked hard to do that and I'm
21 eager to get any kind of help I can get. And I mean
22 that.

EXHIBIT
B

CLOSING - EXCERPT   3/2/2015

Page 41

1 of by the benefactor that has made herself available
2 to help Ms. Hill and I'd ask you to do that as soon
3 as practicable.
4   In addition, we have to have the 24-hour a
5 day home healthcare available. Again, Ms. Caldwell,
6 I would ask that you help us out in finding an
7 appropriate healthcare company, an appropriate
8 provider, and an appropriate regimen, whether it's
9 people on 12-hour shifts, whether it's somebody that
10 lives there, whether it's appropriate to -- I'll
11 call them baby monitors, there is probably a better
12 word for it. But whatever needs to be done, if you
13 could work with the healthcare provider and get from
14 them an estimate.
15   MR. LABOWITZ: You're talking about when
16 Ms. Hill returns to Alexandria, is that correct?
17   THE COURT: Yeah.
18   MR. LABOWITZ: Okay.
19   THE COURT: Get from them an estimate as to
20 what their fees are going to be, get something in
21 writing from them and I'm going to require that Cher
22 pay into Mr. Chew's trust account or Ms. Niesen's

Page 42

1 trust account -- I'll leave it to you all as to what
2 you think is best -- enough funds to cover two years
3 of healthcare going forward from the time that
4 Ms. Hill gets here, so that there won't be any
5 question about them getting paid if there is some
6 change in circumstance with -- with the benefactor.
7   There is some question about what is
8 appropriate in terms of family visitations coming to
9 the home. Ms. Caldwell, again, I don't mean to put
10 it on you, but I'm going to ask that -- that when
11 the family wants to visit, at least in the initial
12 term, that they get in touch with you and you tell
13 them, okay, you can come, I'm going to notify the
14 home healthcare provider that you're coming, and
15 make those visits.
16   If there is a suggestion that Ms. Hill
17 should be taken out of the house for lunch or
18 something, I'm going to leave it to your good
19 judgment to determine whether that's appropriate and
20 Ms. Caldwell can have the final say on that. And if
21 there is a question about it, we can come back here.
22   There is also the issue of -- there are

Page 43

1 three professionals here who have -- who have put in
2 tremendous time and tremendous effort and tremendous
3 skill, quite frankly, in getting this case resolved.
4 I don't think it's fair to any of them for their
5 good works to go uncompensated any further.
6   So either we need to make provisions to
7 take out a second trust or another loan on the house
8 or if the benefactor who is -- who has come forward
9 on these other matters would be willing to front the
10 money and put a lien on the house with the
11 understanding that it be repaid when the house
12 eventually is sold. But one of the conditions is
13 these folks get paid.
14   And I will ask each of you to submit a --
15 your complete invoice to Mr. Chew so he could
16 forward along to Cher and figure out if that's
17 something -- if we can do it that way or if we have
18 to get a second loan on the house.
19   Ms. Hill should have -- certainly
20 telephonic access to all family members while she's
21 in Florida and while she's here.
22   Mr. Chew is right, you know, this is about

Page 44

1 Ms. Hill's well-being, it's not about making a
2 spectacle of her life, and if -- if there's going to
3 be filming, if there's going to be documentaries, I
4 just don't know that there is anything that could
5 come out of a documentary that would be in
6 Ms. Hill's best interest. There may be other folks
7 who have some interest in that, but there's not
8 going to be any more filming of Ms. Hill until
9 further order of the Court.
10   Is that all? Have I left something out?
11   MS. NIESEN: Your Honor, if her income does
12 not substantiate a second mortgage on the house --
13   THE COURT: If that's going to be a
14 problem, then we're going to have to figure out
15 another way to do it. That's going to have to be
16 either through the benefactor or through a second
17 trust or whatever -- whatever other creative way you
18 all can come up with, but these folks need to be
19 paid.
20   MR. CHEW: Understand, Your Honor. May we
21 submit a proposed order tomorrow since we have a
22 court reporter to --

Casamo & Associates   703 837   www.casamo.com

home (are Estimate

I recommend Mrs. Hill have a live-in caregiver (Certified Nursing Assistant) and in addition to this an 8-hour caregiver (Certified Nursing Assistant) overnight to allow the live-in caregiver to receive 8 hours of uninterrupted sleep. This will provide more continuity of care and is more cost effective than 2 twelve-hour shifts and even with the Fair Labor Standards Act change.

Ready Hands Home Care, Licensed and bonded
$235.00-$300.00 Live-In (may increase due to Fair Labor Standards Act)
$22.00   Hourly

Synergy Home Care, Licensed and bonded
$240.00-$300.00 Live-in
$23.00   Hourly

Old Dominion Home Care, Licensed and bonded
$240.00-$300.00 Live-In
$23.00   Hourly

Live-in Certified Nursing Assistant Average $300.00 X 365 days = $109,500.00

Hourly over night Certified Nursing Assistant Average $23.00 X 8 = 184 X 365 days = $67,160

Total per year for home care on average: $176,660.00
$50.00 a week for food for live in caregiver $2,600.00

Care Management Services:

Drafting a working Plan of Care $1,200

Providing ongoing care management services $155.00 an hour
Providing Emergency services if needed $155.00-$232.00 (off hours)

I believe the first two months will be the most time intensive then things should (hopefully calm down).
I would estimate $4,500-$5,000 for the first two months and 3,500 or less there after.
Total per year for Care Management: 45,000 or less

ElderTree Care Management Services
www.ElderTreecare.com/ 703-424-   Office

Document 22
Last will and testament of Edith H. hill

This is the revised Last Will and Testament that Rebecca edited. While she altered certain provisions, she retained the clause confirming that our mother intended for me to serve as executor following Uncle Hubbard.

LAST WILL AND TESTAMENT

OF

EDITH H. HILL

I, EDITH H. HILL, of   Street, Alexandria, Virginia   , being of sound and disposing mind and memory, do hereby make, publish and declare this to be my Last Will and Testament:

ARTICLE I

I hereby revoke all wills and codicils heretofore made by me.

ARTICLE II

I hereby appoint my brother, CURTIS L. HUBBARD, of Silver Spring, Maryland, Executor of this my Last Will and Testament, and I direct that he shall not be required to give bond or security in any jurisdiction for the faithful performance of his duties, any statute to the contrary notwithstanding.

In the event that my brother, CURTIS L. HUBBARD, should predecease me or fail to qualify or having qualified should die, resign, or cease or become incapacitated to act as Executor hereunder, then my daughter, PATRICIA E. BARBER, shall serve in his place and stead as Executor hereunder, and I direct that she shall not be required to give bond for the faithful performance of her duties, any statute to the contrary notwithstanding.

ARTICLE III

I direct my Executor to pay all of my just debts, funeral expenses, including for a suitable marker or monument for my grave, and costs of administration as soon after my death as may be practicable, except that the payment of any debts secured by a mortgage or pledge of real or personal property may be postponed. I further direct that should any real property pass by operation of law or be distributed in kind upon which there is a debt secured by mortgage, deed of trust, or other security agreement, that the property shall pass subject to that debt, and my estate shall not be liable to pay the same.

ARTICLE IV

1. I give and bequeath my home at   Street, Alexandria, Virginia   , to all of my children equally to share and share alike, namely:

   a. My daughter, PATRICIA E. BARBER
   b. My son, LEWIS E. McDANIEL
   c. My daughter, CHRISTINA ROSENBERG
   d. My daughter, REBECCA M. WRIGHT
   e. WILLIAM DALTON HILL, the son of my late husband, WILLIAM E. HILL.

2. I direct that my issue, PATRICIA E. BARBER, LEWIS E. McDANIEL, CHRISTINA ROSENBERG, and REBECCA M. WRIGHT, shall inherit my aforementioned home, per stirpes, meaning that if any of them shall predecease me, then that particular child's interest in my property shall be distributed to their descendants equally.

3. I direct, however, that if WILLIAM DALTON HILL, the son of my late husband should predecease me, then his interest in my home shall go to my above named issue and no distribution shall be made to his descendants or estate.

ARTICLE V

I give and bequeath to CHARLOTTE PHILLIPS, of Omaha, Nebraska, the daughter of my late husband, WILLIAM E. HILL, the sum of FIVE THOUSAND DOLLARS ($5,000.00). If she should predecease me, this money should not be distributed to her descendants or estate, but should remain a part of my estate.

ARTICLE VI

All the rest, residue and remainder of my estate, of every kind and description, wherever situate and howsoever held, I give, devise and bequeath to my issue who survive me, per stirpes, to share and share alike equally.

ARTICLE VII

1. Whenever the words "issue," "descendants" or words of similar purport are used herein, the same shall also include a person related by or through adoption as if the person were related by or through birth, except that a person who is adopted after he or she has attained eighteen (18) years of age and descendants of such person shall not be so included.

2. Whenever herein there is to be a division among or distribution to or for the benefit of issue per stirpes living at any specified time, the property shall be divided into as many equal shares as are necessary to provide one share for each then living child of such person and one share collectively for the then living issue of each child of such person who is then deceased leaving one or more issue then living, such issue to take per stirpes the share which their ancestor, such deceased child, would have taken if he or she had then been living.

ARTICLE VIII

In managing and administering any and all assets of my estate, I hereby give and grant to my Executor, in addition to all other powers granted by law, all powers, authorities and discretions set forth in Section 64.1-57 of the Code of Virginia as in force on the date of the execution hereof, which powers are hereby incorporated by reference and made a part hereof; it being intended my intention to give to my Executor full management and control of my estate, such powers being by way of illustration and not by way of limitation.

IN WITNESS WHEREOF, I have hereunto set my hand and affixed my seal this 16th day of December, 2006, to this my Last Will and Testament.

Edith H Hill
EDITH H. HILL

Robert E Wright
Witness

Ave.
Address

_Alton A___
Witness

Falls Church, VA
Address

Burke VA

STATE OF VIRGINIA
COUNTY/CITY OF _Fairfax_

Before me, the undersigned authority, on this day personally appeared EDITH H. HILL, _Robert E. Wright_, and _Althea Harris_, known to me to be the testator and the witnesses, respectively, whose names are signed to the foregoing instrument and, all of these persons being by me first duly sworn, EDITH H. HILL, the testator, declared to me and to the witnesses in my presence that such instrument is her last will and testament and that she had willingly signed and executed it in the presence of said witnesses as her free and voluntary act for the purposes therein expressed; that said witnesses stated before me that the foregoing will was executed and acknowledged by the testator as her last will and testament in the presence of said witnesses who, in her presence and at her request, and in the presence of each other, did subscribe their names thereto as attesting witnesses on the day of the date of said will, and that the testator, at the time of the execution of said will, was over the age of eighteen years and of sound and disposing mind and memory.

Edith H Hill
Testator

Robert E. Wright
Witness

Althea Harris
Witness

Subscribed, sworn and acknowledged before me by EDITH H. HILL, the testator, and subscribed and sworn before me by _Robert E. Wright_ and _Althea Harris_ witnesses, this _16th_ day of _December_, 2006.

Long D. Phan
Notary Public

My Commission expires: _April 30, 2010_

LONG D. PHAN
Notary Public
Commonwealth of Virginia
My Commission Expires Apr 30, 2010

Document 23
Defendant Cher's memorandum in support of demurrer to the complaint

This is a court record containing Cher's defense argument in response to my lawsuit. The record indicates that, under Virginia law-where the filming occurred-a documentary is not required to be entirely factual, provided it includes a newsworthy element.

VIRGINIA:

IN THE CIRCUIT COURT FOR THE CITY OF ALEXANDRIA

PATRICIA BARBER, et al.,   )
)
                    Plaintiffs,   )
)
v.   )   Case No.:
)   CL18001993
KARTEMQUIN FILMS, LTD., et al.,   )
)
                    Defendants   )

DEFENDANT CHER'S MEMORANDUM IN SUPPORT OF DEMURRER TO THE COMPLAINT

Defendant Cher, by and through her undersigned counsel, hereby submits the following memorandum in support of her Demurrer to the Complaint (filed yesterday, June 27, 2018).

I. INTRODUCTION

This action stems from the making of the documentary film *Edith+Eddie* (2017). Patricia Barber, individually and as Administrator of the Estate of Edith Hubbard Hill ("Plaintiffs"), alleges, *inter alia*, the unlawful use of Plaintiffs' names, portraits, and pictures without their written consent for the purposes of advertising and trade in violation of Va. Code § 8.01-40. It is well established under Virginia law that the prohibitions in Va. Code § 8.01-40 do not apply to "matters of public interest" or "items that are 'newsworthy'"[1] like those depicted in the documentary. *See Williams v. Newsweek, Inc.*, 63 F. Supp. 2d 734, 736 (E.D. Va. 1999); *WJLA-TV v. Levin*, 264 Va. 140, 161 (2002); *Berger v. Capitol Color Mail, Inc.*, 38 Va. Cir. 261 (1995); *see also Messenger v. Gruner+Jahr Printing and Publishing*, 727 N.E.2d 549 (N.Y. 2000) (where the New York Court of Appeals reiterated its long-standing position that the right of privacy statute does not extend "to reports of newsworthy events or matters of public

---

[1] This is generally referred to as the "newsworthiness exception."

interest").[2] As discussed in further detail below, *Edith+Eddie* undoubtedly tells a story that is newsworthy and provides a social commentary that is within the public interest.

Plaintiffs further alleged that Kartemquin Films, Ltd., Heart is Red, LLC, Laura Checkoway, Cher, and Rebecca M. Wright (collectively, "Defendants"), conspired and acted in concert together for the purpose of willfully and maliciously injuring Plaintiffs. Plaintiffs have failed to plead sufficient facts to establish a claim for conspiracy.

II. FACTUAL BACKGROUND

Edith+Eddie tells the story of America's oldest interracial newlyweds -- Edith Hill and Eddie Harrison married at ages 96 and 95, respectively.[3] They had met ten years earlier while playing the lottery in Virginia and described their meeting as "love at first sight." The documentary portrays the life that Edith and Eddie shared together in their home -- doing light exercises, helping and guiding one another through daily activities, and generally discussing their lives. It also captures what Eddie proclaimed to be a "nightmare" when a disagreement arises among Edith's daughters about what is best for their 96 year-old mother with mild dementia. Plaintiff Patricia Barber felt that her mother should be removed from her home with Eddie and

---

[2] Virginia's privacy statute is based on New York state's statute, and accordingly, Virginia courts will often look to New York court decisions in interpreting Va. Code § 8.01-40. *See e.g. Barker v. Richmond Newspapers, Inc.*, 14 Va. Cir. 421 (1973) (noting that "Since our statute was taken from the New York statute (Section 51 of the Civil Rights Law, Consol. Laws, c. 6), the strict construction placed thereon by the New York courts is most persuasive authority in Virginia"); *Town & Country Properties, Inc. v. Riggins*, 249 Va. 387, 394 (1995) (noting that "Code § 8.01-40(A) is substantially similar to §§ 50 and 51 of the New York Civil Rights Act. N.Y. Civ.Rights Law §§ 50-51 (McKinney 1992). Therefore, as we interpret the statute in connection with the constitutional attack, we will look to New York courts for guidance"); *Williams*, 63 F. Supp. 2d at 736 (noting that "There is very little Virginia case law construing this provision, so courts applying Virginia law have relied upon the interpretation of the similarly-phrased New York law as conducted by New York Courts for guidance in construing this provision").

[3] This Court may properly consider the documentary in considering this Demurrer as it is central to the allegations in Plaintiffs' Complaint. *See Dodge v. Trustees of Randolph-Macon Woman's Coll.*, 276 Va. 1, 5 (2008) (noting that a circuit court considering a demurrer may consider "the terms of authentic, unambiguous documents that properly are a part of the pleadings"); *see also Williams*, 63 F. Supp. 2d at 736 (noting that the court may consider as part of the complaint the magazine article and photograph alleged to have violated Va. Code § 8.01-40 at the motion to dismiss stage, even though they were "beyond the pleadings"); *Candelaria v. Spurlock*, No. 08 CIV. 1830 BMCRER, 2008 WL 2640471, at *1 (E.D.N.Y. July 3, 2008) (where the court watched the documentary and discussed the specific clip at issue: "From my viewing of the film and the specific clip at issue…"). The documentary is available for free public viewing at https://www.youtube.com/watch?v=RBNLxU98svQ. Thus, this is not a speaking demurrer.

placed under her care in Florida, while Defendant Rebecca Wright fought to keep Edith together with Eddie. Ultimately, the Court appointed a third-party guardian for Edith. The guardian, having never met Edith, showed up one rainy night with the police and Ms. Barber and removed Edith from her home with promises to Eddie that Edith would return in two weeks. Eddie was unable to reach Edith during that time but eagerly awaited her return. When Edith did not return, Eddie collapsed and passed away shortly thereafter.

The 29-minute documentary won multiple awards and earned an Oscar nomination. It tells a compelling story about love and tragedy -- that love knows no age or race, while also detailing the challenges of caring for the elderly and the strife that it can lead to amongst family members. Moreover, the documentary explores the guardianship system and prompted a dialogue around elder rights and guardianship reform.

Plaintiffs filed a Complaint containing three Counts: Count I seeks monetary damages for an alleged violation of Va. Code § 8.01-40; Count II seeks a preliminary and permanent injunction to prevent the documentary from being shown; and Count III seeks monetary damages for an alleged Conspiracy to injure the Plaintiffs, all of which fail to state a claim upon which relief can be granted.

III. LEGAL STANDARD

"In any suit in equity or action at law, the contention that a pleading does not state a cause of action or that such pleading fails to state facts upon which the relief demanded can be granted may be made by demurrer." Va. Code Ann. § 8.01-273. The standard of review applicable to a circuit court's decision to sustain a demurrer is well established. "A demurrer accepts as true all facts properly pled, as well as reasonable inferences from those facts." *Steward v. Holland Family Props., LLC*, 284 Va. 282, 286 (2012). However, a demurrer "does not admit the correctness of the conclusions of law stated by the pleader. Nor does a demurrer admit 'inferences or conclusions from facts not stated.'" *See Arlington Yellow Cab Co. v. Transportation, Inc.*, 207 Va. 313, 319 (1966) (internal citations omitted). At the demurrer stage, it is not the function of the circuit court to decide the merits of the allegations set forth in a complaint, but only to determine whether the factual allegations pled are sufficient to state a cause of action. *See Riverview Farm Assocs. Va. Gen. P'ship v. Bd. of Supervisors of Charles County*, 259 Va. 419, 427 (2000). Virginia courts have sustained demurrers under the newsworthiness exception to Va. Code § 8.01-40. *See e.g. Graham v. Young Broad. of Richmond, Inc.*, 60 Va. Cir. 376 (2002) (holding that "The court agrees with the defendants that the reporting on a local car dealership issue is a newsworthy item and of public interest. Therefore, the court sustains the demurrer as to the Va.Code § 8.01–40 claim.").

IV. ARGUMENT

A. *Edith+Eddie* Falls Within the Newsworthiness Exception to Va. Code § 8.01-40.

Virginia does not recognize a common law right of privacy. *See Falwell v. Penthouse Int'l, Ltd.*, 521 F. Supp. 1204, 1210 (W.D. Va. 1981) (noting that "Virginia has never recognized a common law cause of action for invasion of privacy"); *see also WJLA-TV*, 264 Va. at 160, n. 5. 161. Rather, Virginia is one of the few states, along with New York, that has codified the common law right of privacy. It has done so in Va. Code § 8.01-40, which provides in relevant part:

> Any person whose name, portrait, or picture is used without having first obtained the written consent of such person, or if dead, of the surviving consort and if none, of the next of kin, or if a minor, the written consent of his or her parent or guardian, **for advertising purposes or for the purposes of trade**, such persons may maintain a suit in equity against the person, firm, or corporation so using such person's name, portrait, or picture to prevent and restrain the use thereof; and may also sue and recover damages for any injuries sustained by reason of such use. And if the defendant shall have knowingly

used such person's name, portrait or picture in such manner as is forbidden or declared to be unlawful by this chapter, the jury, in its discretion, may award punitive damages.

Va. Code § 8.01-40(A) (emphasis added).

Because Va. Code § 8.01-40 is in derogation of the common law, the Court must strictly construe it. *See Falwell*, 521 F. Supp. at 1210. "Therefore, plaintiff must satisfy each of the statutory prerequisites, including the requirement that plaintiff's name or likeness be used for purposes of advertising or trade." *See id.*; *see also Candelaria v. Spurlock*, No. 08 CIV. 1830 BMCRER, 2008 WL 2640471, at *1 (E.D.N.Y. July 3, 2008) (noting that to state a claim under the New York privacy statute, "a plaintiff must allege: (1) the use of his name, portrait, or likeness; (2) for 'advertising purposes or for the purposes of trade;' (3) without written permission.").

Discussion under Virginia law about what constitutes "advertising" or "trade" purposes is limited. *See Berger v. Capitol Color Mail, Inc.*, 38 Va. Cir. 261 (1995) ("What constitutes use of a picture for 'purposes of trade' is not expressly defined by the statute"); *but see Town & Country Properties, Inc. v. Riggins*, 249 Va. 387, 395 (1995) (noting that "a name is used 'for advertising purposes' when 'it appears in a publication which, taken in its entirety, was distributed for use in, or as part of, an advertisement or solicitation for patronage of a particular product or service.'") (citations omitted). It should be noted that just because a film is created with profit in mind, it does not follow that the film was created for purposes of trade:

> Obviously, everything that appears in a magazine is placed with the intention of increasing sales. But if the "purposes of trade" requirement were to be so broadly construed, it would conflict with the limited legislative goal in enacting a statute that creates a cause of action which did not exist at common law. Such an unnecessarily broad construction would likewise intrude on important constitutional freedoms, which guarantee the uninhibited dissemination of ideas.

See Falwell, 521 F. Supp. at 1210; *see also Williams*, 63 F. Supp. 2d at 737 (rejecting argument that defendant was liable under Va. Code § 8.01-40 following plaintiff's assertion that article was for advertising purposes "because it was intended to boost sales"); *Messenger ex rel. Messenger v. Gruner + Jahr Printing & Pub.*, 94 N.Y.2d 436, 442 (2000) (noting that "the fact that a publication may have used a person's name or likeness 'solely or primarily to increase the circulation' of a newsworthy article—and thus to increase profits—does not mean that the name or likeness has been used for trade purposes within the meaning of the statute.").

However, regardless of the meanings of "advertising" or "trade" purposes, it is well settled under Virginia law that Va. Code § 8.01-40 does *not* apply to items that are "newsworthy" or "matters of public interest." *See WJLA-TV*, 264 Va. at 161; *Williams*, 63 F. Supp. 2d at 736. Matters which are newsworthy or of public interest are not considered to be used for advertising or trade purposes. *See Dallesandro v. Henry Holt & Co.*, 166 N.Y.S.2d 805, 806 (1957); *Finger v. Omni Publications Int'l, Ltd.*, 564 N.Y.S.2d 1014 (1990). The newsworthiness exception is "designed to balance the need for the dissemination of news and information against an individual's right to control the use of his likeness." *Williams*, 63 F. Supp. 2d at 736. In light of the significant constitutional concerns associated with limiting First Amendment speech and press rights, courts have regularly held that the terms "newsworthy" and "public interest" are to be broadly construed and liberally defined. *See e.g. Messenger ex rel. Messenger v. Gruner + Jahr Printing & Pub.*, 94 N.Y.2d 436, 441–42 (2000) (noting that "this Court has held that 'newsworthiness' is to be broadly construed. Newsworthiness includes not only descriptions of actual events but also articles concerning political happenings, social trends or any subject of public interest") (internal citations omitted); *Arrington v. New York Times Co.*, 55 N.Y.2d 433, 440 (1982) (noting that "public interest" is "clearly a term to be freely defined"); *Delan by Delan v. CBS, Inc.*, 458 N.Y.S.2d 608, 613 (1983) (noting that "matters of public interest" include items which "are designed to be informative"); *Gaeta v. Home Box Office*, 645

N.Y.S.2d 707, 709 (Civ. Ct. 1996) (noting that "The term public interest has been 'liberally applied' or 'freely defined,' in recognition of 'Federal and State constitutional concerns for free dissemination of news and other matters of interest to the public.'"). "The question of whether something is newsworthy is a question of law for the courts to decide." *Candelaria*, 2008 WL 2640471 at *2 (citing to *Lemerond*, 2008 WL 918579, at *2). In determining whether an item is newsworthy, courts consider solely the "content" of the film in question, not the producer's "motive to increase circulation." *See id.* "Furthermore, courts should be wary not to 'supplant the editorial judgment of the media in determining what is 'newsworthy' or of 'public interest.' Consequently, 'public interest' and 'newsworthy' have 'been defined in most liberal and far reaching terms.'" *Id.* (citation omitted).

Edith+Eddie clearly falls within the newsworthiness exception to Va. Code § 8.01-40. The documentary tells a compelling story about finding love at an age that few people would ever imagine, which in itself is newsworthy. Even more significantly, the documentary presents a commentary on several matters of public interest (a term that is to be broadly defined), including interracial marriage, elder rights, elder care, intra-family disputes, and the guardianship system. For example, the documentary delivers subtle criticisms of the guardianship system: "The guardian is now in control of Edith's life and is compensated through Edith's estate. The guardian has never met Edith"[4] and "Edith's guardian…becomes legally responsible for Eddie's remains. To this day, no memorial plans have been made."[5] The documentary also serves to educate and inform the general public on issues about which they may not be aware, as evidenced by the moment when Edith and Eddie struggle to grasp the reality of the power the guardian has over Edith, with Eddie asking the guardian "Can you forcibly take her out of her

---

[4] *See* documentary at 6:11 mark.
[5] *See* documentary at 28:02 mark.

own home?" to which the guardian replies "I can..."[6] These are clearly matters of public interest in line with other documentaries where courts have dismissed invasion of privacy claims. *See Candelaria*, 2008 WL 2640471 at *4 (holding with respect to the documentary *Super Size Me* that "Having considered these principles and cases, it is clear that the movie here meets both the newsworthiness and incidental use exceptions to NYCRL § 51, The movie aims to educate and address in detail the obesity epidemic and related health risks associated with eating fast-food. The fact that this movie garnered so much attention and earned a profit is of no moment"); *Delan*, 458 N.Y.S.2d at 613 (holding that "In our opinion, the documentary film with which this case is concerned dealt with a matter of legitimate public interest, i.e., the deinstitutionalization of mental patients and their placement in an outpatient program designed to benefit both themselves and society as a whole. It involved a critical review of the mental hygiene program in this State as a matter of general and public concern, and the telecast, therefore, was clearly a privileged subject.").

Like the documentaries in *Candelaria* and *Delan*, *Edith+Eddie* provides a commentary on legitimate matters of public interest and it further informs the general public about issues of which many are not aware. Accordingly, Plaintiffs' claim for invasion of privacy in Count I must fail. Plaintiffs' Complaint fails to state facts upon which an invasion of privacy can be premised because Plaintiffs failed to show that Cher's actions were for advertising or trade purposes.

To the extent Plaintiffs' claims in Count I are based on a "false and negative depiction in the Film" (*see e.g.* Complaint ¶ 23, *see also* Complaint ¶ 12), Plaintiffs claim must fail because Virginia does not recognize a claim for false light invasion of privacy. *See WJLA-TV*, 264 Va. at 160 (noting that "The common law torts of invasion of privacy are (1) unreasonable intrusion upon the plaintiff's seclusion, or solitude, or into his private affairs; (2) public disclosure of true,

---
[6] *See* documentary at 18:13 mark.

embarrassing private facts about the plaintiff; (3) publicity which places the plaintiff in a false light in the public eye; and (4) misappropriation of plaintiff's name or likeness for commercial purposes. By codifying only the last of these torts, the General Assembly has implicitly excluded the remaining three as actionable torts in Virginia. Accordingly, we agree with WJLA and the amici curiae that, to the extent that count five asserts a claim for false light publicity, it fails to state a proper cause of action") (internal citations omitted); *see also Falwell*, 521 F. Supp. at 1206 (noting that "Plaintiff's claim for 'false light' invasion of privacy must be dismissed as a matter of law. The courts of Virginia simply do not recognize such a common law cause of action."). Cher's Demurrer should be granted.

B. Plaintiffs Are Not Entitled to a Preliminary or Permanent Injunction.

Plaintiffs' requests for a preliminary and permanent injunction also stem from Va. Code § 8.01-40, which provides for injunctive relief ("...such persons may maintain a suit in equity against the person, firm, or corporation so using such person's name, portrait, or picture to prevent and restrain the use thereof..."). However, because there is no underlying violation of Va. Code § 8.01-40, as discussed in Section A, *infra*, there is no activity to enjoin and Plaintiffs' request for injunctive relief must be denied.

Further, the Supreme Court has found that restraining speech prior to a final determination that the speech is not protected is an unconstitutional and invalid prior restraint on the exercise of First Amendment rights. *See Vance v. Universal Amusement Co.*, 445 U.S. 308, 316 (1980). Any prior restraint on expression comes "with a 'heavy presumption' against its constitutional validity." *See Org. for a Better Austin v. Keefe*, 402 U.S. 415, 419 (1971). Preliminary and permanent injunctions are both examples of prior restraints. *See Alexander v. U.S.*, 509 U.S. 544, 550 (1993). The problem with prior restraints (and especially preliminary injunctions), as determined by courts across this country, is that they enjoin potentially protected speech prior to an adjudication on the merits of the speaker's First Amendment rights. *See e.g. Pittsburgh Press Co. v. Pittsburgh Comm'n on Human Relations*, 413 U.S. 376, 390 (1973) (noting that "The special vice of a prior restraint is that communication will be suppressed, either directly or by inducing excessive caution in the speaker, before an adequate determination that it is unprotected by the First Amendment."). It makes no difference that the Plaintiffs have alleged the film places them in a negative light. *See Org. for a Better Austin*, 402 U.S. at 419 (noting that "No prior decisions support the claim that the interest of an individual in being free from public criticism of his business practices in pamphlets or leaflets warrants use of the injunctive power of a court."). For this additional reason, Defendant's Demurrer should be sustained with respect to Count II in the Plaintiffs' Complaint.

C. The Court Should Sustain Cher's Demurrer with respect to Count III Because Plaintiffs Have Failed to Plead Sufficient Facts to Support a Claim for Conspiracy.

Under Virginia law, Plaintiffs must satisfy four elements to state a *prima facie* case for common law conspiracy. *See Commercial Bus. Sys., Inc. v. Bellsouth Servs., Inc.*, 249 Va. 39, 48 (1995) (noting that "A common law conspiracy consists of [1] two or more persons combined [2] to accomplish, by some concerted action, [3] some criminal or unlawful purpose or some lawful purpose by a criminal or unlawful means. [4] The foundation of a civil action of conspiracy is the damage caused by the acts committed in furtherance of the conspiracy.") (internal citations omitted). The Supreme Court of Virginia has recognized that "a common law claim of civil conspiracy generally requires proof that the underlying tort was committed." *See Almy v. Grisham*, 273 Va. 68, 80 (2007). As discussed in Section A, *infra*, Plaintiffs have failed to allege facts sufficient to establish a violation of Va. Code § 8.01-40. Accordingly, Plaintiffs' Count III Conspiracy claim should be rejected and Defendant's Demurrer granted.

Further, Plaintiffs have failed to plead sufficient facts to survive this Demurrer. "Virginia requires a plaintiff to allege 'some details of time and place and the alleged effect of the conspiracy.'" *Firestone v. Wiley*, 485 F. Supp. 2d 694, 704 (E.D. Va. 2007) (citing to *Johnson v. Kaugars*, 14 Va. Cir. 172, 176 (Va. Cir.1988)). A complaint which "contains only conclusory or general allegations of conspiracy" is "insufficient to withstand a motion to dismiss." *See id.* Where there are only "vague, conclusory allegations of conspiracy, the claim fails at the threshold." *See id.* Here, Plaintiffs have alleged nothing more than the conclusory allegations which have been deemed insufficient under Virginia law. *See* Complaint ¶¶ 31-33.

V. CONCLUSION

For all of the reasons stated above, Defendant Cher respectfully requests that this Court sustain her Demurrer, dismiss the Complaint with prejudice, and grant such further relief that it deems appropriate.

Dated: June 28, 2018

Respectfully submitted,

Benjamin G. Chew, VSB No. 29113
Andrew C. Crawford, VSB No. 89093
BROWN RUDNICK LLP
, NW, Suite
Washington, DC
(p): 202-536-
(f): 617-289-
BChew@   .com

Counsel for Defendant Cher

www.ingramcontent.com/pod-product-compliance
Lightning Source LLC
Chambersburg PA
CBHW070337240426
43665CB00045B/2166